KATE CHOPIN

A Study of the Short Fiction

Also available in Twayne's Studies in Short Fiction Series

Twayne's Studies in Short Fiction

Gordon Weaver, General Editor
Oklahoma State University

KATE O'FLAHERTY—LATER KATE CHOPIN—IN 1869, AT AGE 19, ABOUT THE AGE OF EUPHRASIE MANTON IN "A NO-ACCOUNT CREOLE," THE FIRST STORY IN *BAYOU FOLK*, CHOPIN'S FIRST BOOK OF SHORT STORIES. *(Missouri Historical Society)*

KATE CHOPIN
A Study of the Short Fiction

Bernard Koloski
Mansfield University of Pennsylvania

TWAYNE PUBLISHERS
An Imprint of Simon & Schuster Macmillan
New York

PRENTICE HALL INTERNATIONAL
London Mexico City New Delhi Singapore Sydney Toronto

Twayne's Studies in Short Fiction Series, No. 65

Copyright © 1996 by Twayne Publishers

Twayne Publishers
An Imprint of Simon & Schuster Macmillan
1633 Broadway
New York, New York 10019

Library of Congress Cataloging-in-Publication Data
Koloski, Bernard, 1937–
    Kate Chopin : a study of the short fiction / Bernard Koloski.
        p.   cm. — (Twayne's studies in short fiction : no. 65)
    Includes bibliographical references (p.   ).
    ISBN 0-8057-0865-0
    1. Chopin, Kate, 1851–1904—Criticism and interpretation.
    2. Women and literature—Louisiana—History—19th century.
    3. Louisiana—In literature.   4. Short Story.   I. Title.
    II. Series.
    PS1294.C63K65   1996
    813'.4—dc20   96-31123
                                                            CIP

The paper used in this publication meets the minimum requirements of American National Standard for Information Sciences—Permanence of Paper for Printed Library Materials. ANSI Z39.48-1984. ∞™

10 9 8 7 6 5 4 3 2

Printed in the United States of America

For Monique

Contents

Contents

Preface

Kate Chopin was bilingual and bicultural. She was born in the United States and left the country only once, on her wedding trip through western Europe, but she spoke French as well as English throughout her life, translated French fiction into English, and functioned within two quite different cultures—wealthy, sophisticated, English-speaking communities in St. Louis, New Orleans, and northwestern Louisiana, and wealthy, sophisticated, French-speaking communities in those areas. Her bilingualism, biculturalism, and life among intelligent, questioning people are central sources of the extraordinary freedom and originality, the unique vision and mode of expression that characterize her work.

The two novels and the hundred short stories she wrote in St. Louis between 1888 and 1904 carry the literary markings of the times, of the American local-color movement and the international realistic and naturalistic movements. They deal for the most part with everyday, contemporary life. They are set more often than not in Louisiana, where Chopin spent her married years, and emphasize the languages and dialects spoken by people in the area. Most are what realists would call "objective" in their presentation—observational, with the author's personality hidden—and are expressed in language that is simple and clear. Many are sympathetic pictures of common people, often people from the lowest social classes in the South. Some stress the deterministic effects of heredity and environment.

But Kate Chopin was never much at ease with her literary contemporaries or with the theories or goals of the movements many of them helped bring about. Neither was she at ease with the earlier romantic writers whom the realists and naturalists had supplanted or with the authors of the popular domestic novels, the sentimental novels, so common in the United States through most of the nineteenth century. She took what she needed from the currents of her times, enough to place her stories in the best magazines—*Vogue*, the *Atlantic Monthly*, the *Century*, *Harper's Young People*, *Youth's Companion*, and others. She reached back to the romantics, to Walt Whitman in particular, for imagery and rhythm. She drew inspiration from French opera and theater and used techniques of the sentimental novelists when that suited her purposes. She read widely but was influenced mostly by French writers, Guy de Maupassant more than any other.

Her subject matter grew rather directly out of her life, as Emily Toth, her recent biographer, has shown.[1] She was reasonably prosperous by the standards of St. Louis or New Orleans and lived a reasonably happy, fulfilling life, but she knew pain and hardship. Her father died when she was five, her half brother when she was 13, and her husband when she was 32. She bore the trauma of being a Confederate sympathizer during the Civil War, of watching her husband's business fail and her life in New Orleans collapse, and of having her novel, *The Awakening*, condemned by influential critics. And through 14 years of daily contact with some of the struggling urban and rural people of Louisiana—Creoles, Acadians, African Americans, Hispanics, Native Americans, mixed breeds, rich and poor, young and old—she understood something of poverty, illiteracy, and violence.

She grew up among single, independent women, spending much of her youth with her mother, grandmother, and great-grandmother, so she was especially aware of the social possibilities for women and makes exploration of those possibilities the subject of some of her most powerful fiction—*The Awakening* and stories like "A Respectable Woman," "Athénaïse," "The Story of an Hour," and "A Pair of Silk Stockings." Her stories about women have for 25 years driven the remarkable revival of her work and placed her in the first rank of American writers.

Yet Kate Chopin is not a one-subject author. Her focus on gender is a component of her more comprehensive sensitivity of vision. Like many women writers of her time, she has an understanding of women's ambivalent struggle for autonomy, individual identity, and self-fulfillment, on the one hand, and for continued possibilities of marriage and motherhood, on the other. But because she was bilingual, bicultural, and sophisticated in her thought she has, unlike most of her contemporaries, a feel for the ways that socialization—a person's language, culture, and economic and social environment—shapes that struggle. And because she had known such personal pain and had lived and worked among so many different people, she identifies women's struggles with those of others who are dominated, dispossessed, or striving—reading one in the light of the other, illuminating the yearnings of one by the experience of the other.

Many of her short stories deal with such yearnings, her people—in particular her young people—trying to maintain or, more often, to achieve a social position from which their needs and desires might be satisfied. Louisiana in Kate Chopin's work is a setting for struggles among individuals seeking better social possibilities for themselves. Yet Chopin would have been contemptuous of efforts to identify her fiction with ideological movements for social change. Although she is emphatically a product of nineteenth-century America and a writer of stories for American readers, she wanted her work to be measured by historical and international standards. She rebukes her fellow American Hamlin Garland for insisting in his *Crumbling Idols* that writers restrict themselves to present-day concerns:

> Human impulses do not change and can not so long as men and women continue to stand in the relation to one another which they have occupied since our knowledge of their existence began. It is why Æschylus is true, and Shakespeare is true to-day, and why Ibsen will not be true in some remote to-morrow, however forcible and representative he may be for the hour, because he takes for his themes social problems which by their very nature are mutable. And, not withstanding Mr. Garland's opinion to the contrary, social problems, social environments, local color and the rest of it are not *of themselves* motives to insure the survival of a writer who employs them.[2]

Kate Chopin did not write in service of an ideology. She wrote the strongest, most original fiction she knew how and created some of the most vibrantly alive characters in nineteenth-century American literature, among them Edna Pontellier in *The Awakening*, Athénaïse Miché and her husband Cazeau in "Athénaïse," Mrs. Baroda in "A Respectable Woman," the boy in "A Vocation and a Voice," and the lovers Calixta and Alcée in "At the 'Cadian Ball" and "The Storm." She asked that her work be judged not by what it does but by what it is, not by whether it changes the world but by whether it is "true life and true art," as she phrases it in her first critical essay, whether it shows "human existence in its subtle, complex, true meaning, stripped of the veil with which ethical and conventional standards have draped it" (691–92).

This volume seeks to read Kate Chopin's fiction with that request in mind. It is different in several ways from previous studies. It focuses exclusively on the short stories and examines those stories in the context of Chopin's bilingual and bicultural imagination. It introduces readers to the hundred-year-long discussion of the works. And it points to aspects of Kate Chopin's fiction that bring readers new insight at the turn of the twenty-first century.

Part 1 offers an introduction to Chopin's short fiction and suggests readings of her strongest stories. It describes Chopin's three volumes of short stories, her 30 or so children's stories, and a few of her uncollected stories, revealing the basic contours of Chopin's writing career—her early exuberance, her mature balance, her late disillusionment. Part 1 is not much concerned with questions of gender. For 25 years other critics have set forth forcefully, at times brilliantly, the role of gender in Chopin's short fiction. Some of their work is included in Part 3 of this volume and listed in the bibliography.

Part 2 presents samples of Chopin's literary criticism, selections from essays that document her beliefs about what literature should be and do.

Part 3 contains critical essays by Chopin scholars. Each essay concentrates on a particular story, group of stories, or volume of stories.

Notes

1. Emily Toth, *Kate Chopin* (New York: William Morrow, 1990), 35; hereafter cited in the text.

2. Per Seyersted, ed., *The Complete Works of Kate Chopin*, 2 vols. (Baton Rouge: Louisiana State University Press, 1969), 693. All further quotations from Chopin's works are cited in the text as page numbers only. Pagination runs consecutively through the two-volume *Complete Works*.

Acknowledgments

I acknowledge with thanks the right to reprint material from several sources.

In Part 2, Kate Chopin's "Confidences" reprinted by permission of Louisiana State University Press from *The Complete Works of Kate Chopin, Volume II*, edited by Per Seyersted. © 1969 by Louisiana State University Press.

In Part 3:

From Anna Shannon Elfenbein, *Women on the Color Line: Evolving Stereotypes and the Writings of George Washington Cable, Grace King, and Kate Chopin* (Charlottesville: University Press of Virginia, 1989), 126–31. Used by permission of the University Press of Virginia.

From Susan Lohafer, reprinted by permission of Louisiana State University Press from *Coming to Terms with the Short Story*, by Susan Lohafer. © 1983 by Louisiana State University Press.

From Peggy Skaggs, reprinted by permission of Twayne Publishers, an imprint of Simon & Schuster Macmillan, from *Kate Chopin*, by Peggy Skaggs. © 1985 by G. K. Hall & Co.

From Mary E. Papke, *Verging on the Abyss: The Social Fiction of Kate Chopin and Edith Wharton* (Westport, CT: Greenwood Press, 1990), 62–64. © 1990 by Mary E. Papke. Reprinted with permission of Greenwood Publishing Group, Inc. All rights reserved.

From Emily Toth, © 1995 by Emily Toth.

From Barbara C. Ewell, excerpts from *Kate Chopin*, by Barbara C. Ewell. © 1986 by the Ungar Publishing Company. Reprinted by permission.

From Per Seyersted, *Kate Chopin: A Critical Biography*. © 1969 by Per Seyersted.

I am grateful to many people whose work or friendship has influenced this study:

Emily Toth, whose Chopin biography and good advice have been invaluable,

Acknowledgments

Chopin scholars Per Seyersted, Barbara Ewell, Thomas Bonner, Jr., Peggy Skaggs, Joyce Dyer, Mary Papke, Patricia Lattin, and Robert Arner, whose books and essays I have turned to again and again,

French sociologist Pierre Bourdieu, whose insights I have drawn from throughout this study,

Carolyn Heilbrun, Peggy Skaggs, and Joseph Gibaldi, whose acts of kindness some years ago have helped my work along,

Gordon Weaver, the general editor of this Twayne series, who has been gracious and supportive,

Larry Uffelman, Jay Gertzman, Jim Glimm, Judith Sornberger, John Ulrich, Lynne Pifer, Tom Murphy, and Walter Sanders, whose judgments have been helpful,

Priscilla Older, Boyd Collins, Larry Schankeman, and Jeanne Fessenden of the Mansfield University Library, Sion M. Honea of the Sibley Music Library at the Eastman School of Music, reference librarians at the Pennsylvania State University Library, and the staff of the Bibliothèque Municipale de Toulouse, in France, who guided me to materials,

Bronwyn Medland and Lisa White, who helped transfer Chopin's short fiction into electronic form,

Juliane Longenbach, who helped verify the accuracy of details,

Dick Walker and Yvonne Harhigh,

My daughters Milissa, Laurie, and Jenny,

And, more than anyone else, Monique Oyallon, who introduced me to Pierre Bourdieu and offered countless suggestions throughout the writing of this book.

Part 1

THE SHORT FICTION

Introduction

In "The Story of an Hour" (written in 1894),[1] one of Kate Chopin's best-known short stories, Mrs. Mallard sits alone in a locked room gazing out her open window at a patch of blue sky and the tops of trees bursting with new growth. She smells rain in the spring air and hears sparrows on the roof above her, a peddler in the street below, and someone singing off in the distance. She has just been told—very gently, because she has a heart condition—that her husband was killed in a train crash. She has sobbed with grief in her sister's arms, then retreated alone to her room where, still sobbing at times, she sits now in her armchair facing the window.

"There was something coming to her," Kate Chopin writes, "and she was waiting for it," something "too subtle and elusive to name," something "creeping out of the sky, reaching toward her through the sounds, the scents, the color that filled the air." She tries to push away "this thing that was approaching to possess her," to "beat it back with her will," but she cannot. She yields to it—and a "little whispered word" escapes her lips. She repeats it "over and over under her breath: 'free, free, free!' " (353).

It is a powerful moment, a startling moment, one of the most heavily discussed moments in nineteenth-century American literature. Scores of critics have described it as a woman's cry of joy over liberation from male dominance. Mrs. Mallard's husband had "never looked save with love" upon his wife, Chopin writes, yet he has a "powerful will" capable of "bending hers," which is "a crime," whether the intention is "kind" or "cruel," so Mrs. Mallard's face has lines that "bespoke repression." Now she is suddenly free of him, and even though she "had loved him—sometimes" and knows she will "weep again" when she sees "the kind, tender hands folded in death," she knows too that her life has been transformed. Now she will "live for herself," not for her husband (353). Reprinted in countless paperback anthologies and college textbooks, "The Story of an Hour" is one of America's most successful short stories.

It is also a fine introduction to the imaginative universe of Kate Chopin's short fiction, a universe governed by a vision that is informed, intelligent, and compassionate, sensitive to ambiguity, far ahead of its time in the late nineteenth century and, in ways, still ahead of its time today.[2] "The Story of an Hour" is itself in large part about vision, about what Mrs. Mallard sees, about what the story's narrator sees that Mrs. Mallard sees. For 17 of the story's 23 paragraphs, Mrs. Mallard sits in her armchair staring out the window. In the last three paragraphs she stands up "with a feverish triumph in her eyes," walks down the stairs, and, when she sees her husband come in the door, dies of heart failure. The words *eyes, look, see, saw, stare, view, gaze,* and *glance* appear more than a dozen times in this story of just over a thousand words.

Mrs. Mallard is focused on her husband's repression of her, a man's repression of a woman. But the narrator—and, perhaps, Mrs. Mallard as well—understands such repression in a larger context. Mrs. Mallard now "would live for herself," the story reads. "There would be no powerful will bending hers in that blind persistence with which *men and women* believe they have a right to impose a private will upon a fellow-creature" (353; emphasis added).

To "live for herself," to live free of coercion by another, is Mrs. Mallard's hope—and the hope of many people inhabiting Kate Chopin's world. An instinctive yearning for freedom, for a more fulfilling life, is an organizing theme in *The Awakening* (1899) and in some of Chopin's strongest short stories. But in almost all these narratives, there is an additional context—something within the story itself, something in the relation of a story to another story, something in the reappearance of a person from an earlier story. The narrator in "The Story of an Hour" steps back at a "brief moment of illumination," a moment of intense emotional sensation, to find in the events taking place a more complex perspective, to notice that women as well as men "believe they have a right" to coerce others. A slight phrase, a small detail, carries that perspective.

Critics by the 1960s and the early 1970s—before most Americans had heard of *The Awakening*—were sensitive to the subtlety of Chopin's vision and mode of expression. Kenneth Eble, who in 1964 edited the first paperback version of *The Awakening*, helping to set off the Chopin revival in the United States, speaks of Kate Chopin's "underground imagination"—"the imaginative life which seems to have gone on from early childhood somewhat beneath and apart from her well-regulated actual existence."[3] Daniel Aaron adds that Chopin had "what Hawthorne called 'the hawk-eye.' That is to say, she was observant and detached. She displayed quite early a sense of irony toward herself and the world."[4] George Arms argues that Chopin "presents a series of events in which the truth is present, but with a philosophical pragmatism she is unwilling to extract a final truth. Rather, she sees truth as constantly re-forming itself and as so much a part of the context of what happens that it can never be final or for that matter abstractly stated."[5]

A sense of distance, irony, and context are present throughout Kate Chopin's work. Chopin grew up in St. Louis and wrote all her fiction there—yet her stories are set mostly in Louisiana. She was a rather prosperous woman who knew good food, clothing, housing, conveniences, even cigarettes, who owned property and traveled abroad—yet her fictional world is rife with poverty and illiteracy. She was a sophisticate, a widely read, cultivated woman who loved theater, music, and opera, whose circle of friends monitored intellectual and cultural influences flowing from Europe through the work of Sigmund Freud, Charles Darwin, Karl Marx, and others—yet many of the most memorable characters in her stories are simple people, products of a rural, provincial life.

The Literary Field in Chopin's Time

Chopin could publish short stories about poor people, simple people, Louisiana people because of the nature and the economics of the literary field in St. Louis and the United States in the 1880s and 1890s. It was an age of narrative prose appearing in literary and popular magazines and newspapers. Several thousand magazines were being published in the country in the 1890s, many of them directed at women and children. A large number of Americans, many if not most of them women, wrote fiction and poetry for these popular periodicals. Regional fiction, local color fiction, was in demand.

The greater part of the magazines and newspapers were regional, as all periodicals had been earlier in the century. Chopin published some of her stories in *St. Louis Life, St. Louis Magazine,* the St. Louis *Mirror* or *Criterion* or *Spectator*—she had hired a St. Louis publisher, Nixon-Jones, to publish her early novel, *At Fault* (1890)—or in the New Orleans *Times-Democrat*. But by the 1890s there were national literary magazines and newspapers as well. Chopin placed other stories in *Two Tales, Vogue,* the *Century* (formerly *Scribner's Monthly,* which also published in serial form Mark Twain's *The Adventures of Huckleberry Finn* and Henry James's *The Bostonians*), the *Atlantic Monthly,* the *Saturday Evening Post, Youth's Compan-*

ion, and *Harper's Young People*—published mostly in the East. Houghton Mifflin, the publisher of Chopin's first collection of short stories, was in Boston and New York. Way and Williams, the publisher of her second, was in Chicago, as was Herbert S. Stone, the publisher of *The Awakening*. Kate Chopin's first book of short stories, *Bayou Folk*, appeared in 1894. *A Night in Acadie* was published in 1897. Chopin set out plans for a third volume, to be called *A Vocation and a Voice*, that would have appeared in 1900 or 1901, but for reasons not well understood, the publisher canceled the book. It was published as a separate volume only in 1991.[6]

Realism: Maupassant, James, and Zola

The short fiction Chopin wrote bears the markings of other authors of her times. She knew and loved the poems of Walt Whitman; she read and praised the work of American writers Sarah Orne Jewett, Mary Wilkins Freeman, and Ruth McEnery Stuart; and she was familiar with the writing of many other Americans. Her vision shares a good deal with that of her contemporary Henry James. But the strongest influences on her work came from European writers.

Guy de Maupassant (1850–1893), born the same year as Chopin, was a revelation for her. She studied his stories, translated several into English, and absorbed what attracted her: "direct and simple" phrasing (701), an economy of detail, a penchant for ironic endings, and a fascination with—a continual focus on—the way that women respond to the people around them.

It is difficult to overemphasize the effect of Guy de Maupassant on Kate Chopin. Realism was in the air when Chopin started to write. A generation of writers in both Europe and America had eagerly turned away from the romantic tendency to picture human beings as unique, free individuals and were describing people instead as shaped by social, biological, economic, and other forces and struggling to maintain some individuality and freedom by confronting those forces. Maupassant, more than anyone else—except, perhaps, the Russian Anton Chekhov—showed the world how to express such a view of life in short fiction. He created a language for the short story, a way of speaking that sounded like the truth of life, as informed people at the time understood life.[7] Kate Chopin approached that language in its original French and, drawing on her acquaintance with French culture, felt its spirit and force. Maupassant's markings are everywhere in her work.

The American realist Henry James (1843–1916) read Guy de Maupassant at about the same time as Kate Chopin did and at about the same point in his life (Chopin was seven years younger than James), and both wrote down their reactions in the mid-1880s. The two found Maupassant enormously effective, a master, incomparable. Both understood that he was not only extraordinarily gifted but also that he wrote, as James says, "directly *from*" his gifts, that he holds "the fullest, the most uninterrupted . . . the boldest communication with them."[8]

Unlike French authors, James says, English or American writers "are apt to be misled by some convention or other as to the sort of feeler we *ought* to put forth, forgetting that the best one will be the one that nature happens to have given us" (James, 249). Chopin senses something similar. "Here was a man," she writes, "who had escaped from tradition and authority, who had entered into himself and looked out upon life through his own being and with his own eyes; and who, in a direct and simple way, told us what he saw. When a man does this, he gives us the best that he can" (701).

Yet while they share an admiration for, a sense of awe about, what Maupassant has accomplished, James is uncomfortable with matters that Chopin is not. Maupassant sees life as a "terribly ugly business," though "relieved by the comical," James argues. "Almost all" his characters are driven by a "sexual impulse," his women are "detestable," and, most importantly, he "has simply skipped the whole reflective part of his men and women—that reflective part which governs conduct and produces character" (James, 266, 258, 276, 285). If any of these matters bothers Kate Chopin, she does not show it. "I read his stories and marvelled," she writes. "Here was life, not fiction" (700).

The effect of the naturalist Émile Zola (1840–1902) on her is more complex. Critics have generally assumed Chopin disliked Zola because she complains in a review of his novel *Lourdes* (1894) that the book is a "mistake" in its treatment, that it is full of "prosaic data, offensive and nauseous description and rampant sentimentality," and that it is openly designed to instruct (697). Yet her review shows she knew Zola well, was familiar with his work—that is, with some of his famous *Rougon-Macquart* novels, published between 1871 and 1893, and perhaps something of his very early work—and trusted the validity of his insights:

> I once heard a devotee of impressionism admit, in looking at a picture
> by Monet, that, while he himself had never seen in nature the peculiar

yellows and reds therein depicted, he was convinced that Monet had painted them because he saw them and because they were true. With something of a kindred faith in the sincerity of all Mons. Zola's work, I am yet not at all times ready to admit its truth, which is only equivalent to saying that our points of view differ, that truth rests upon a shifting basis and is apt to be kaleidoscopic. (697)

The image of a kaleidoscope emphasizes the centrality of vision for Kate Chopin, the importance of seeing the truth. She could offer no higher praise to Zola than that his vision is truthful, even if she is sensitive to patterns created by aspects of the truth different from those he is looking at from where he stands. Chopin dislikes *Lourdes* and faults it for moralizing, but she respects Zola's earlier works, the best known of which (in her time and ours) are 20 novels that chronicle life in Second-Empire France (1852–70), a period of great material prosperity. It is not clear what Chopin might have found in whatever she read, but Zola's disgust with the wastefulness, corruption, and ruthless social climbing by all classes of French society permeates the *Rougon-Macquart* novels, as does his disdain for the adultery and sexual promiscuity he sees all around him.[9]

Most of Zola's Second-Empire people are seeking in whatever way they can to cash in on the enormous new wealth generated by the era's quick industrial growth. Certainly Louisiana as Kate Chopin knew it in the 1870s was anything but prosperous. Her Southerners are trying their best only to preserve—or to enhance a little—whatever they have in a region still not recovered from the devastation of the Civil War. The materialism so despised by Zola has no parallel in Chopin's world.

Yet her fiction, like Zola's, is regularly focused on the way that people shaped by their social environment seek to carve out better lives for themselves. And like Zola's stories, Chopin's deal openly with people's sexuality. The patterns Chopin sees in her kaleidoscope are brighter, more hopeful than those Zola discerns—people in Chopin's world have an even chance of being successful at finding a better life; sex for them is life-affirming rather than corruptive—but many of the elements out of which those patterns emerge are similar. The influence of Zola, like that of Maupassant, is evident throughout Chopin's work.

Language and Culture

Although she was affected by what she read, Kate Chopin's short stories emerged from the two languages and cultures she functioned within.

Scholars say that bilingualism is not unusual, that more than half the people alive today are bilingual, having, to some extent, a native ability to speak in two languages.[10] The 1899 *Encyclopedia of the History of St. Louis* notes that Chopin used French before English, "French being the language spoken in her family in those days."[11] Chopin was—in good part because of the work of her maternal great-grandmother—"always at home in French," as Emily Toth, her recent biographer, shows (Toth, 35).[12] Her stories are full of French phrases and of expressions that blend French with English, that render French in English.

Chopin could have been bilingual without being bicultural, but she was both. The older French families in the St. Louis of Kate Chopin's youth shared their Catholicism with the new Irish immigrants in the city—Kate Chopin's mother came from French stock, her father was Irish—but considered the newcomers a class below themselves. The French had quite different notions of food, clothing, beauty, politeness, success, authority, power, change, work, prestige—all the dispositions that a person assimilates by living in a culture, a community of people who share a language, a set of beliefs, values, feelings, a group identity. Chopin learned to shift back and forth between cultures in St. Louis, as well as between languages. She did the same in New Orleans, when she moved there after her marriage, and later in northwestern Louisiana, where she lived for five years and where many of her stories are set. The great critic Edmund Wilson writes that Chopin's style combines "French limpidity with Irish grace."[13]

Her subject matter often draws power from the positioning of one culture alongside another. Her fiction is similar in that respect to the work of Henry James. But James's great theme is international, Chopin's is intercultural. In much of his best work, James explores the consequences of socialization by positioning Americans among Europeans. In much of hers, Chopin positions Protestants among Catholics (the Presbyterian Edna Pontellier, for example, among the Catholics at Grand Isle), blacks among whites, 'Cadians among Creoles, the dominated among the dominant, those coming into their own among those losing what they have.

James's people are often intensely aware of much of what they do. Many of them live carefully examined lives. A few of Chopin's people do. But most—Mrs. Mallard in "The Story of an Hour" among them—live by the instincts, the dispositions, the inclinations, the tastes they have received from the people around them, from the groups within which they function.[14]

Louisiana: Creoles and 'Cadians

Kate Chopin lived in Louisiana for fourteen years. She spent nine years in New Orleans—from 1870, when she married Oscar Chopin and moved with him to the city, to 1879, when Oscar's business failed. She spent five years in Cloutierville, near Natchitoches, in northwestern Louisiana—from 1879 when she moved there with Oscar to manage some plantations and run a general store, to 1884, two years after Oscar died, when she returned to St. Louis. Much of her fiction captures what she must have observed during those fourteen years.

New Orleans in the 1870s was a city of foreigners and immigrants. According to the *Statistical Atlas of the United States* based on the 1870 census, more than 25 people per square mile were of foreign birth, with 20 to 30 percent of the aggregate population of the city being foreign, a percentage higher than anywhere in the South at the time.[15] So Kate Chopin found in New Orleans in the 1870s a city with a higher proportion of foreigners—of immigrants and children of immigrants—than she had known in her native St. Louis, higher than almost anywhere else in the South, and about as high as anywhere else in the United States. She found also a city—and a state—still devastated by the effects of the Civil War. About a third of the prewar wealth had disappeared in Louisiana, per capita income had declined precipitously, plantations were in ruins, racial tensions were high, violence was pervasive. And, Kate Chopin learned, people in the state spoke and acted in different ways.

Mark Twain explains at the beginning of *Huckleberry Finn* that he has carefully distinguished among the dialects he uses in the book. "I make this explanation," he adds, "for the reason that without it many readers would suppose that all these characters were trying to talk alike and not succeeding."[16] Readers new to Kate Chopin might well suppose that her characters were doing the same. Her stories are populated by Creoles, 'Cadians, African Americans, Native Americans, Hispanics, and people of mixed blood.[17] The characters not only speak in distinct ways but also lead lives quite different from one another.

Chopin's Creoles are descendants of Catholic French or Spanish settlers. Though most of them sustained terrible Civil War losses from which they have not recovered, they are likely to be educated, cultured landowners or merchants. The older Creoles in the stories speak a dialectal French among themselves and maintain as much of their European culture as they can. Their sons and daughters are more likely to speak English among themselves. Larzer Ziff describes Chopin's Creoles in cogent detail:

> The community about which she wrote was one in which respectable women took wine with their dinner and brandy after it, smoked cigarettes, played Chopin sonatas, and listened to the men tell risqué stories. It was, in short, far more French than American, and Mrs. Chopin reproduced this little world with no specific intent to shock or make a point. . . . Rather, these were for Mrs. Chopin the conditions of civility, and, since they were so French, a magazine public accustomed to accepting naughtiness from that quarter and taking pleasure in it on those terms raised no protest. But for Mrs. Chopin they were only outward signs of a culture that was hers and had its inner effects in the moral make-up of her characters.[18]

Chopin's Acadians—'Cadians or Cajuns—are descendants of the two or three thousand Catholic exiles from Acadia, Nova Scotia, whose long journey to Louisiana was celebrated by Henry Wadsworth Longfellow in his narrative poem *Evangeline* (1847). After the British drove out these French-Canadians in 1755, most found their way to Bayou Teche and Bayou Lafourche.[19] Poorer and less well educated than the Creoles—but also speaking a dialectal French—the 'Cadians eke out an existence from the land by fishing, farming, and hiring themselves out to the wealthier Creoles.

Just below the surface of many Chopin stories is an unrelenting poverty, a stark illiteracy, and a potential for violence. Although nobody in the stories seems to be starving, several people, like Lalie in "Love on the Bon-Dieu," look like they lack "wholesome and plentiful nourishment" (153), and Lolotte in "A Rude Awakening" has nothing but corn bread and pork to feed her sick brother. Many people are clad in rags and live in ramshackle cabins or shacks. Even most of the formerly grand plantation houses are in a state of near ruin, with dilapidated galleries, crumbling porticos, and leaking roofs.

Many of Chopin's people are illiterate, and some of the women are physically abused. 'Tite Reine of "In Sabine" cannot flee from her lazy, drunken, abusive husband because she does not know how to read and write and cannot appeal for help. Telésphore Baquette of "A Night in Acadie" has made himself literate because his uncle—against whom he defines himself—is illiterate. Zaïda Trodon of the same story escapes marriage to a man no better than 'Tite Reine's husband only because a young farmer happens to be present at a critical moment and is strong enough to physically drive off the would-be abuser. Deadly or near-deadly confrontations are present in "A No-Account Creole" and the novel *At Fault* and are threatened in "Athénaïse" and "In and Out of Old Natchitoches." Many people in New Orleans and those on vacation on Grand Isle live very well indeed, but the economic condition of most people in Chopin's upstate Louisiana is desperate.

Regionalism and Local Color

From her first published story to her last, Kate Chopin was thought of in her own times as a regionalist, a local-color writer, an artist committed to capturing in prose the folkways and speech patterns of Louisiana. Modern readers often understand local colorists as closer to historians than to novelists or short-story writers, as lesser artists focused on surface characteristics, as less earnest, less serious than other realists.

Kate Chopin certainly did not see herself as a lesser writer. The Creoles in her stories embody, as Nina Baym points out, "not only a past that was quickly fading away, but a present that America had never chosen to embrace. Their lives could be presented as more pleasure-oriented, more easygoing, more gracious, and more sensuous than those of the mainstream Americans who would in all probability be reading about them. And while they were rural, they still had a European sophistication which might well be beyond that of the average American; where most local color characters were more primitive than the assumed reader, the Creole was in many ways more sophisticated."[20]

Chopin wrote for a national audience and sought wide recognition, and today what she had set out to do seems quite clear. For generations, readers have understood local color as motivated by an author's desire to preserve for posterity a way of life that was disappearing. But local-color fiction has always been more complex and less benign.

Local-color writers, like regionalists in other art forms, make people "see and believe," help them "know and recognize," as French sociologist Pierre Bourdieu has shown,[21] and in doing so not only affirm the local culture they are describing but also confront the larger, dominant society they are writing for. By arguing to preserve a physical place, a social space, for a culture, local colorists urge a society to make room for it, to integrate it into the whole, to give it a better position than it would have if their fiction had not been written or read. And because they present themselves as interpreters of that culture, they seek a more valued place for themselves, as well.

It is such a sense of possession, of repossession, that flows through Chopin's short fiction—mostly Southern, mostly rural, mostly poor, mostly female. Chopin offers her readers not an ideology, not a coherent system for remaking the social world, but a strategy, a way of working with what she has, of bringing to life what she knows. The people in her imaginative world reach for better social positions. Kate Chopin seeks an enhanced position for them—and, as importantly, for herself—through her fiction about them.

Bayou Folk

Bayou Folk (1894) is a young person's book. Its best stories are about people in their late teens or their twenties—people setting out in life, seeking occupations and companions for themselves. Many of the older people in the volume are looking back at their youth, remembering, or trying to remember, or paralyzed by the memory of, what life was like when they were young, often striving to re-create the conditions of their youth. About half of the 23 stories in the volume are directed to children.

In its opening story and some other stories, *Bayou Folk* is optimistic, hopeful, not because it sentimentalizes life or ignores reality—it deals with some painful material: racial prejudice, poverty, violence, desertion, abuse, insanity—but because the stories are charged with the energy of youth, with an unspoken, at times a childlike, determination to make the best of things, to reach for as much as can be grasped, to plunge into life without much concern about dangers that might lie ahead.

But sometimes *Bayou Folk* is hesitant and tentative. People in some stories pull back from the possibility of achieving better lives. They retreat into their fears or memories, into the safety of their families or communities.

And when it takes up people's lifelong obsessions, especially obsessions with race, when it focuses on white people's inability to identify with the plight of black people, *Bayou Folk* becomes sour, despondent, pessimistic.

The seven or eight best stories in the volume reflect all of these moods.

"A No-Account Creole"

"A No-Account Creole" is Kate Chopin's first story and one of her most important ones, begun in 1888 when Chopin was 38 and finished three years later. It is the first of her stories published in a national magazine—the *Century* for January 1894—and it is the first story in *Bayou Folk,* her first book of stories.[22]

It is about an instinctual preference for harmonious balance, about 18-year-old Euphrasie Manton's deeply socialized disposition toward a life of rich possibilities. A house suggests Euphrasie's yearning for a better life. Chopin will use a house to embody such a yearning again and again in her short work, and Edna Pontellier in *The Awakening* will leave her husband's house and move into a rented "pigeon house" where she can seek greater autonomy.

The house in "A No-Account Creole" is the Santien place, built by one of the great families in Chopin's world. Santiens appear in Chopin's early novel *At Fault,* in the first three stories in *Bayou Folk,* and in "Ma'ame Pélagie." The house rests on a thousand-acre plantation near the Red River in northern Louisiana, where Euphrasie lives with her father Pierre, the caretaker. The two subsist in poverty because the once magnificent plantation had been destroyed during the Civil War and the three Santien boys, inheritors of the land, have yielded ownership to their New Orleans creditors.

Euphrasie had agreed to marry Placide, the youngest Santien, who lives in "a little shell of a house" (84) in a neighboring village and ekes out a living by painting other people's homes. She "saw no reason why she should not be his wife when he asked her to" (86), but her heart is not in the engagement, though from infancy she has loved Placide as a big brother. Eight years earlier, when her mother died, she had been taken to live at Les Chêniers, the plantation of Mme. Duplan, "the Lady Bountiful of the parish," who lived "en grand seigneur" (84, 85). There Euphrasie developed the very dispositions that Placide has come to reject bitterly because he has neither the means nor the energy to reclaim and restore his family's plantation.

Euphrasie has lived two lives—one with the Duplans, who have a great many privileges, and one with her father, who has few. She returns to her father after eight years with the Duplans because she cannot let him alone on the run-down plantation, and she behaves in such a way that "no one could have guessed" she had any regrets about leaving the wealthy family (86) because Creoles such as the Duplans and the Santiens value the ability to bear misfortune with silence and grace. An old man in "At the 'Cadian Ball" later in *Bayou Folk* finds it "altogether chic, mais chic" that a rich planter shows no reaction whatsoever after a cyclone destroys his 900 acres of rice (223).

It is easy for a modern reader to miss Chopin's intention with the house imagery, to identify Euphrasie and characters in later stories with those countless lost Southerners who wander through American fiction of the last 150 years, seeking to construct some imagined ideal life that they believe was destroyed by the Civil War and that they associate with magnificent columned plantation mansions. Chopin understands the type—she will create a representative in "Ma'ame Pélagie"—but Euphrasie is not lost and not, like some other people in *Bayou Folk*, seeking a fantasy.

Like so many of Chopin's Louisiana people, Euphrasie does not consciously grasp what she wants, but Wallace Offdean, the man Euphrasie falls in love with and, we presume, eventually marries, certainly does. Although "A No-Account Creole" is about Euphrasie's choice of a husband and a way of life, Chopin begins the story with the focus on Wallace Offdean.

"He was a sure-footed fellow, this young Offdean," Chopin writes, "despite an occasional fall in slippery places. What he wanted, now that he had reached his twenty-sixth year and his inheritance, was to get his feet well planted on solid ground, and to keep his head cool and clear" (81). The specifics of Offdean's agenda that Chopin offers in these first pages of her first story speak persuasively to Americans at the turn of the twenty-first century: "With his early youth he had had certain shadowy intentions of shaping his life on intellectual lines. That is, he wanted to; and he meant to use his faculties intelligently, which means more than is at once apparent. Above all, he would keep clear of the maelstroms of sordid work and senseless pleasure in which the average American business man may be said alternately to exist, and which reduce him, naturally, to a rather ragged condition of soul" (81).

Offdean belongs to "good society" and is possessed of "healthy instincts" (81), resembling, perhaps, Kate Chopin's husband, as biographers suggest. When the New Orleans creditors send Offdean to the old plantation to see whether it can be sold, he grasps immediately the charm of the place along with the charm of Euphrasie; as the two explore the house and the land and its people, they recognize each other as kindred spirits, drawn together by "instincts" they have learned from experiencing the potential of life in "good society." Their love for each other emerges from a shared vision of the balance, the harmony that could be theirs on the plantation.

They do not dream of midnight balls or uniformed servants. Offdean has a "beggarly" $25,000 inheritance (80), sufficient to buy the land and make a start on some improvements, but not enough to live in luxury. It is balance he wants: "He saw the whole delicious future which a kind fate had mapped out for him: those rich acres upon the Red River his own, bought and embellished with his inheritance; and Euphrasie, whom he loved, his wife and companion throughout a life such as he knew now he had craved for,—a life that, imposing bodily activity, admits the intellectual repose in which thought unfolds" (97).

Euphrasie and Offdean each brings something to their marriage—she a firm grasp of what it is possible to do with the plantation and the practical knowledge to get it done, he some financial resources and a conscious determination to face the future with his eyes open. The quality of life that they reach for together reverberates throughout Kate Chopin's stories. It offers a standard against which other lives and other stories can be measured.

"Ma'ame Pélagie"

Like "A No-Account Creole," "Ma'ame Pélagie" (1892) is about a yearning for life in a plantation manor, but the hopes of Euphrasie and Pélagie and the outcomes of those hopes could hardly be more different. Euphrasie looks to the future, Pélagie to the past. Euphrasie seeks a happy life, Pélagie a happy death. Euphrasie succeeds, Pélagie fails.

In both stories, the narrative revolves around the reconstruction of a house. Pélagie Valmêt remembers her life in the "imposing" red-brick manor on the Côte Joyeuse before the war began 30 years ago. She remembers her love for a man named Felix and their hope for marriage, her desolation when Felix leaves for battle, and her dramatic rescue of her five-year-old sister, Pauline, from the manor house set on fire by Yankee soldiers. Now she and Pauline live in poverty in a cabin near the ruined mansion, not because they have no money, but because the 50-year-old Pélagie is obsessed with saving every picayune so that someday—perhaps 20 years from now before she dies, or 40 years from now before Pauline dies—the mansion can be restored to its former glory, its Pantheon-like appearance (232).

The narrative action is set in motion in both stories by the appearance of an outsider who alters the balance of forces that has kept the mansion from being rebuilt.[23] As Wallace Offdean in "A No-Account Creole" stirs hope in Euphrasie, La Petite, the adolescent niece of Pélagie and Pauline in "Ma'ame Pélagie," awakens powerful feelings in the two women. Pauline, now 35, is content to stay with Pélagie because she does not remember the splendor of the manor house, and she has known no other existence than what she has had with her sister. But when La Petite comes to live on Côte Joyeuse one summer, Pauline's steps "grew very buoyant . . . and her eyes were sometimes as bright as a bird's." The appearance of La Petite does for Pauline what life at Les Chêniers does for Euphrasie—it reveals alternatives, and it exposes the "strange, narrow existence," the "dream-life" she lives, for what it is (233–34). The years begin to fall away from Pauline.

In both stories, the outsider articulates the qualities that would constitute a better life. La Petite's cheek that was "tinged like the pink crèpe myrtle" becomes pale "like the creamy plumes of the white crèpe myrtle that grew in the ruin." "I love you both," she tells Pélagie and Pauline, "but I must go away from you. . . . I must live another life; the life I lived before. I want to know things that are happening from day to day over the world, and hear them talked about. I want my music, my books, my companions" (234–35). Pélagie is content. La Petite will distract her from the hope she lives for. But Pauline is devastated. "If La Petite goes away I shall die," she says. "She seems—she seems like a saviour; like one who had come and taken me by the hand and was leading me somewhere—somewhere I want to go" (235).

In "A No-Account Creole," the earlier story, the house itself remains a physical structure. Chopin compares the moss-covered roof to an "extinguisher," something that protects the rooms below (she describes a sunbonnet as an extinguisher in her story "The Bênitous' Slave"); she associates the building with the odors of flowers, and she presents it as it appears to those who love it—charming in spite of its leaky roof and crumbling verandas. It is a shelter for Offdean and Euphrasie, a structure within which they can reach for happiness.

But in "Ma'ame Pélagie" the ruin takes on human or animal qualities. It "brooded like a huge monster," Chopin writes, "a black spot in the darkness that enveloped it" (238). It is for Pélagie a living "dream" (232), a fantasy, one of the many fantasies that haunt people in *Bayou Folk,* and Chopin suggests the nature of the fantasy through the language she uses to describe it.

Pélagie refuses life for herself. She refuses to participate. She wants to reconstruct the manor so she can die in the same room where Felix said good-bye to her. She does not respond to the trumpet vine that now grows in that room. Nevertheless, she razes the structure and builds a "shapely" wooden home so La Petite will stay and Pauline will be happy, because she understands that their life must take precedence over her hope to die in the restored mansion. During the war she had saved Pauline's life. Now she saves it again. Pélagie understands the need for sacrifice (238).

But she knows too that while La Petite and Pauline have gained and will blossom, she has lost and will wither. She has given up her fantasy world, but she has given up something real, as well. Her chance to restore her prewar social position—and the position of her family—is gone. The "shapely" new wooden house is no match for the "imposing" prewar mansion. She has been degraded. She stays dressed in black, and she ages rapidly. "While the outward pressure of a young and joyous existence had forced her footsteps into the light," Chopin writes, "her soul had stayed in the shadow of the ruin" (239).

It is not clear whether Chopin meant for "A No-Account Creole" and "Ma'ame Pélagie" to be read together, but she may have been thinking of the earlier story when she has Pélagie avoid marriage with the father of Placide Santien, the man whom Euphràsie avoids marrying. Pélagie remembers the day when Felix, the man she loves, told her father of his wish to marry her, and she remembers that in the evening Jules Santien—Placide's father—was among the guests at a grand party in the mansion. Jules too wants to marry her. She remembers looking at Jules and wondering if Felix had already told her father of their marriage hopes (236).

"In and Out of Old Natchitoches"

The deep Creole sensitivity to giving scandal, a motif that echoes throughout Chopin's work, including *The Awakening*, is central to "In and Out of Old Natchitoches" (1893). Vintage *Bayou Folk*, the story reinforces the idea of plantation reconstruction, introduces the Laballières—the second of the two great families in the book—and introduces also Athénaïse Miché, on whom Chopin will focus the classic story, "Athénaïse," in her next book, *A Night in Acadie*. "In and Out of Old Natchitoches" is something of a dress rehearsal for the later work, telling of a headstrong young woman who leaves her home in Natchitoches because she cannot bear the presence of a passionate, proud, and arrogant man; settles in a New Orleans boarding house; half falls in love with a sophisticated bachelor; realizes she is making a mistake; and returns to the region and the man she had run from.

Scandal opens the story and closes it. Alphonse Laballière (the quick-tempered brother of Alcée Laballière in "At the 'Cadian Ball"), an outsider who comes to Natchitoches to rebuild a plantation, gets a reputation for liking free mulattoes more than white people. In outraged response to what he says is people's meddling in his private affairs—though he shares most of the racial assumptions of the Creole community—he demands that Suzanne St. Dennis Godolph, who earns her living teaching school in a building on his property, enroll a mulatto in the class, driving her to find employment in New Orleans. Though he scandalizes Suzanne, he quickly sees he has made a fool of himself and alienated the woman he has come to love. But he is in turn scandalized by Suzanne's association in New Orleans with Hector Santien (brother of Placide Santien in "A No-Account Creole"), a notorious gambler. A racial theme is broached here but not developed, as it will be in other Chopin stories.

The narrative includes a lovely, erotic, often-quoted passage in which Hector, admitting to the unbelieving Suzanne—who is half in love with him—that his life is less than respectable, trims a rose with his penknife: "He held the rose by its long, hardy stem, and swept it lightly and caressingly across her forehead, along her cheek, and over her pretty mouth and chin, as a lover might have done with his lips. He noticed how the red rose left a crimson stain behind it" (265).

"In and Out of Old Natchitoches" is the second story in *Bayou Folk*, after "A No-Account Creole," and before "In Sabine." All three stories deal with the Santien brothers—Placide, Grégoire, and Hector.

"At the 'Cadian Ball," "A Visit to Avoyelles," and "In Sabine"

"At the 'Cadian Ball" (1892), one of the strongest stories in *Bayou Folk*, is about choosing marriage partners. The setting where choices are tested is an all-night ball given by 'Cadians. The participants are a wealthy Creole man and woman, a poor 'Cadian man, and a woman of 'Cadian and Cuban ancestry.

A 'Cadian ball is a perfect setting for such a subject and Chopin will use it again in "A Night in Acadie." "Any one who is white may go to a 'Cadian ball," Chopin writes, "but he must pay for his lemonade, his coffee and chicken gumbo. And he must behave himself like a 'Cadian," that is, must cause no disturbances (223). During the long affair, most of the young people dance to the music of black fiddle players while men play cards in a side room, children sleep in *le parc aux petits*, and older people talk in the corners. During breaks in the music, the dancers pour out onto the galleries and to the benches in the shadows to explore possible alliances. At midnight the gumbo is served and the dancing and exploration continues. Only at daylight are pistols fired into the air to announce "*le bal est fini*" (227).

The wealthy planter in the story is a Laballière, one of Chopin's principal Creole families whose members appear in other stories—"Croque-Mitaine," "Loka," "In and Out of Old Natchitoches," "Ozème's Holiday," and "The Storm," Chopin's sequel to "At the 'Cadian Ball." The narrative revolves around the possibility that Alcée Laballière,[24] pursued indirectly by his beautiful Creole kinswoman Clarisse, will pair himself with the mixed-blood Calixta, pursued directly by the 'Cadian Bobinôt.

That Bobinôt should marry Calixta seems natural to the 'Cadians even though Calixta has some Cuban blood (she does not have any black blood) and does not always behave properly in 'Cadian terms, as evidenced by rumors of "scandal" the summer before at her uncle's house in Assumption Parish, when Alcée Laballière was there. "C'est Espagnol, ça," the 'Cadian people say, and because of that Spanish blood, they excuse things in Calixta they would not tolerate in one of their own (219), including her flirting with the Creole Alcée Laballière.

It is not common in Chopin's universe for a 'Cadian woman to pursue a Creole man. Although any of a dozen of the beautiful 'Cadian women would marry Bobinôt, none of them has set her sights on Alcée. Creole women do not go to 'Cadian balls, but Creole men sometimes do, and Alcée Laballière comes to this one because a cyclone has destroyed his 900 acres of rice and because Clarisse has rejected his rough, impetuous declaration of love. He needs a "li'le fling" (222) and hopes to find one by persuading Calixta to revisit her uncle in Assumption.

Like in "A No-Account Creole" and "Ma'ame Pélagie," the appearance of an outsider—in this instance Alcée—sets in motion a change in the balance of social forces that is maintaining the status quo. Bobinôt would in time, it seems, be accepted by Calixta, and Alcée would eventually be accepted by Clarisse, though she does not share his passionate nature and coyly provokes him by receiving suitors from New Orleans. Both alliances are what everyone involved would consider natural.

Both solidify the economic, social, and cultural positions of the four people. An Alcée-Calixta alliance (though not a fling, perhaps all Alcée—and maybe Calixta as well—wants) would be possible but unnatural, elevating the social position of Calixta, depressing that of Alcée, and throwing Clarisse into uncertainty. A Bobinôt-Clarisse alliance is unthinkable. So Alcée's appearance at the ball alarms Bobinôt. It is for the 'Cadian a deeply disturbing act, threatening to cut him off from Calixta and destroy his hopes. It creates a dangerous situation for all four people.[25]

Clarisse understands completely and acts forcefully to intervene. She appears at the ball herself (an unheard-of thing to do), drags Alcée away, and declares her love for him. Calixta sees immediately what has happened, takes Bobinôt off, and tells him she will marry him. Balance is restored. Social position and stability are preserved. The story resembles a Shakespearean comedy.[26]

Two stories, placed earlier in *Bayou Folk* but written after "At the 'Cadian Ball," suggest alternative narratives for a 'Cadian like Bobinôt.

"A Visit to Avoyelles" (1892), written two weeks after "At the 'Cadian Ball," focuses on a 'Cadian man in love with a beautiful woman within the 'Cadian community who would, under ordinary circumstances, marry him, but who is captivated by a handsome outsider. Unfortunately for Doudouce, no second outsider like Clarisse intervenes, so Mentine, the woman he loves, marries Jules, a man from Avoyelles Parish, and, even after seven years, four children, and a life of poverty, remains captivated by him.

Chopin places the narrative not in the neutral territory of a 'Cadian ball at the moment a life decision is being made but at the dilapidated Avoyelles home of the married couple years later. And she does not shift the focus from one person to another, as she does in the earlier story, but keeps it relentlessly on Doudouce who, like Placide in "A No-Account Creole," has reconciled himself to his loss of the woman he loves. Doudouce "held Mentine's happiness above his own." Seeing her for the first time in seven years, he wonders if he would have recognized her outside her home. "He would have known her sweet, cheerful brown eyes, that were not changed; but her figure, that had looked so trim in the wedding gown, was sadly misshapen. She was brown, with skin like parchment, and piteously thin. There were lines, some deep as if old age had cut them, about the eyes and mouth" (228–29).

But Doudouce has not changed his feelings: "He loved her now as he never had. Because she was no longer beautiful, he loved her. Because the delicate bloom of her existence had been rudely brushed away; because she was in a manner fallen; because she was Mentine, he loved her; fiercely, as a mother loves an afflicted child" (231).

"In Sabine" (1893) introduces Placide's brother, Grégoire—a major character in Chopin's early novel *At Fault*—who, like Placide, is unsuccessful in love and who, like Placide and Doudouce, is sensitive to the needs of women, though the married woman whose cabin he comes upon by chance passing through Sabine Parish is not someone he has been in love with. 'Tite Reine, a 'Cadian woman Grégoire had met at a 'Cadian ball, and her husband, Bud Aiken, live in even worse poverty than the couple in "A Visit to Avoyelles." Aiken is one more outsider who captivates and then carries away a strong woman; 'Tite Reine's very name, "little queen," suggests both her imperial manner among family and friends and her determination to choose a mate apart from the men in the community around her. This match, however, has not worked. Her husband drags her from parish to parish, forces her to work in the fields while he drinks, tells her their marriage may not be legitimate, threatens to leave her behind, and beats her. 'Tite Reine is desperate to return to her family, and Grégoire is happy to help her.

Again Chopin sets the narrative in another parish at the miserable cabin of the married couple some time after their marriage and concentrates the narrative on a man apparently rejected by a woman he loves, though it is some nameless woman, not 'Tite Reine, who has rejected Grégoire (*At Fault* offers one possible explanation of what has happened to him). "Grégoire loved women," Chopin writes.

> He liked their nearness, their atmosphere; the tones of their voices and the things they said; their ways of moving and turning about; the brushing of their garments when they passed him by pleased him. He was fleeing now from the pain that a woman had inflicted upon him. When any overpowering sorrow came to Grégoire he felt a singular longing to cross the Sabine River and lose himself in Texas. He had done this once before when his home, the old Santien place, had gone into the hands of creditors. The sight of 'Tite Reine's distress now moved him painfully. (329)

The lines link Grégoire to his brother Placide and the plantation in "A No-Account Creole."

Both "A Visit to Avoyelles" and "In Sabine" focus on a rescuer or, at least, a would-be rescuer, and both introduce a journey motif that Chopin will use again in stories like "Ozème's Holiday" and one of her best works, "A Vocation and a Voice." And "In Sabine" offers an unusual view of race relations. Grégoire helps 'Tite Reine return to her family with the assistance of Uncle Mortimer, a black man who works for Bud Aiken and who once had protected 'Tite Reine from her drunken husband by wielding an ax. As Richard Potter writes, "a black man protecting a white woman is a far cry from the stereotype of the brute Negro ravishing white woman; yet here it is in a story of the 1890s. 'Tite Reine has been saved by a black man, and with Grégoire's help she is finally able to escape, leaving her horseless husband fuming and helpless."[27]

"Désirée's Baby"

L'Abri, the house in the illustrious "Désirée's Baby" (1892), is as menacing as the ruin in "Ma'ame Pélagie" (Chopin wrote the stories within a few months of each other). Despite its name—"the shelter"—L'Abri is not a place of hope, an "extinguisher," as is the house in "A No-Account Creole." Instead its roof "came down steep and black like a cowl," and "solemn" oaks nearby "shadowed it like a pall." Armand Aubigny, Désirée's husband, the young master of L'Abri—the story is one of Chopin's few works set before the Civil War—rules the plantation with an iron hand. Unlike his father, who was "easy-going and indulgent," Armand displays at times "the very spirit of Satan" and the slaves live in fear of him. When Madame Valmondé, who raised the toddler Désirée after someone left her one day on the doorstep, approaches L'Abri to see the mature Désirée, her husband, and their new baby, the house makes her shudder (241–42).

L'Abri dominates the three revelation scenes that constitute the story. It broods over the moment Madame Valmondé first recognizes with a start that Désirée's baby has mixed blood and apparently concludes that Désirée must be part black, because she knows nothing of the foundling's parentage. It is present a month or two later with its "sombre gallery" as Armand tells Désirée that their child is "not white," that *she* is "not white," and that she and the baby should leave. And a few weeks after Désirée and the baby have disappeared, apparently drowned in the bayou, it hovers above the bonfire in the backyard where Armand, trying to cleanse the house of everything belonging to his wife, finds a letter from his mother to his father thanking God their son will never learn—it is the closing sentence of the story—that she herself "belongs to the race that is cursed with the brand of slavery" (243–45). The house is a place of horror, an embodiment of the potential for tragedy inherent in fantasies of racial superiority.

The final sentence is among the most powerful in Kate Chopin's fiction. Not only are Désirée and the baby dead, not only is Armand revealed to be himself what he hatefully accused his wife of being, but the words of revelation come from Armand's mother—a woman with black blood, a woman who lived with her husband the very life that is so impossible for Armand to contemplate, so ugly and unthinkable for him that he must destroy whatever reminds him of it.

Armand's parents had lived in France, not antebellum Louisiana. The story does not say how or where Armand's father and mother met. Monsieur Aubigny had apparently lived in America before having a child—his family was "one of the oldest and proudest in Louisiana." He brought his son "home" from Paris at age eight after his French wife died there (240–41).

Monsieur Aubigny must have fallen in love with Armand's mother "the way all the Aubignys fell in love, as if struck by a pistol shot," and he must have sustained that love throughout their marriage. The part of the old letter that Armand reads at the close of the story begins with his mother "thanking God for the blessing of her husband's love" (240–44). Although it is not clear when or why his wife wrote him that fateful letter, it seems, from all we can tell, that Armand's father knew his wife was black and that the couple lived together openly in Paris. Readers should note that despite what critics and anthologists sometimes assert, the baby and Armand, while part black, are not part African American. Their black blood came to them from Africa by way of France, not the United States. Some of the power of "Désirée's Baby" hinges on differences between cultures. Kate Chopin understood that Parisians during the early decades of the nineteenth century carried racial assumptions of their own but that some kinds of racially mixed alliances might have been socially possible in Paris when they were not in the United States.

"Désirée's Baby" is Kate Chopin's most famous story. It was a success from the moment it appeared in *Vogue* in 1893. By 1907 Leonidas R. Whipple was calling it "one of the most perfect short stories in English."[28] In the 1920s Fred Lewis Pattee, among the first scholars to study the American short story, closed his discussion of the work by writing that Chopin "produced what often are masterpieces before which one can only wonder and conjecture."[29] In the 1930s Arthur Hobson Quinn added his considerable authority to what had become a general opinion among scholars: "Désirée's Baby," he said, is "one of the greatest short stories in the language."[30]

The work appeared in a collection of short stories in 1929, and it has been in print ever since, included today in countless anthologies for the general public, university students, and high school students. With the force of the bonfire at the story's close, "Désirée's Baby" has burned itself into the consciousness of generations of readers. It is among the most powerful condemnations of racism in American literature.

"Madame Célestin's Divorce"

The entire narrative of the witty "Madame Célestin's Divorce" (1893) is played out over a picket fence, a clearly defined boundary between the loquacious Lawyer Paxton (he appears also in "Dead Men's Shoes" and "Tante Cat'rinette") and the pensive Madame Célestin, whose husband has left her and their two children without support for six months. Lawyer Paxton tries his best to lure the pretty Madame Célestin out from behind her fence by urging that she divorce her husband. His intentions are honorable enough. "It would be very good," he dreams, "to take unto himself a wife" (278). But despite standing up to objections from her family, the local priest, and even the bishop—her entire community—Madame Célestin calls off the divorce when her husband returns one night and promises to reform.

Like Lawyer Paxton and Madame Célestin themselves, the story has a flirtatious character—in the charming dialogue, in the descriptions of Madame Célestin in her "snugly fitting calico wrapper," especially "the gray one . . . with a graceful Watteau fold at the back . . . with which she invariably wore a bow of pink ribbon at the throat," and in the picture of the lawyer, who "grew solicitous as to the shine of his boots, his collar, and the set of his tie" (276–78).

Kate Chopin makes much of Madame Célestin's broom, which is present throughout the story. The Creole woman arranges to sweep her gallery each day at the moment the lawyer passes on his way to his office. She balances the broom "gracefully" with one hand as she comes to her picket fence to talk with her confidant, she ends a conversation "with a turn of the head and a flirt of the broom," and she carries the broom the morning she tells the lawyer that her husband came home last night and the divorce is off: "She was making deep rings in the palm of her gloved hand with the end of the broomhandle, and looking at them critically. Her face seemed to the lawyer to be unusually rosy; but maybe it was only the reflection of the pink bow at the throat" (276–79).

The sexual connotations—often apparent in Chopin's stories—suggest the importance of sex among the tools Madame Célestin can muster to attract someone who might help her change her life. The lawyer pursues Madame Célestin, after all, precisely because she is as pretty as the roses Chopin associates her with and because she is skillfully using her sexual power.

But the broom, like the picket fence, suggests also the differences in position of the two people. Lawyer Paxton—from everything we can tell through the three stories he appears in—does not sweep his gallery, wash his shirts, or do other "manual labor" as Madame Célestin does. And he manages his life through secular law—there exists a clear legal basis for a divorce, he argues—while she governs hers through her relatives, her friends, her confessor, and, ultimately, her husband. Lawyer Paxton has thought ahead to the likelihood that should they marry they would leave the community of Louisiana Creoles. "The world was surely wide enough to live in," he concludes. There is no suggestion that Madame Célestin entertains such a possibility (276–78).

Staying with her husband relieves Madame Célestin of the need to venture past her picket fence, to confront her family or church. Sex does more to keep Madame Célestin in her community than to attract someone who might take her out of it. Her boundary remains intact.[31]

"La Belle Zoraïde" and "A Lady of Bayou St. John"

The exuberance and hopefulness of the early stories in *Bayou Folk* are gone by the end of the volume. Two of the last three stories, written within a few weeks of each other, set before and during the Civil War, look back to the earlier "Désirée's Baby" in their treatment of racial prejudice, of white attitudes toward race, but whereas "Désirée's Baby" is scorching, like a bonfire, "La Belle Zoraïde" and "A Lady of Bayou St. John" (both 1893) are caressing, like the distant song that opens "La Belle Zoraïde" or the Creole patois that ends it.

Chopin makes the "music and charm" of the patois essential to "La Belle Zoraïde." They enclose the story of the beautiful slave, Zoraïde, who lapses into insanity when her white mistress blocks her marriage with the black man she loves and takes away their love child (304). But the story's harmonious surface masks a piercing dissonance.

The story is told by old Manna-Loulou, "herself as black as the night" (303), to her young white mistress, Madame Delisle, the title character in "A Lady of Bayou St. John." The beautiful Zoraïde, her skin like café au lait, Manna-Loulou says, had been brought up by Madame Delarivière to be graceful and elegant. Madame was her godmother, as well as her owner, and wanted to ensure a good life for Zoraïde, hoping she would marry "in a way to do honor to" her bringing up—in the New Orleans Cathedral, with a wedding gown and *corbeille* of the best (304). Monsieur Ambroise, a mulatto owned by a friend, was Madame's choice of partner for Zoraïde.

But Zoraïde, Manna-Loulou adds, despised "the little mulatto, with his shining whiskers like a white man's, and his small eyes, that were cruel and false as a snake's" and loved at first sight "le beau Mézor" when she saw him dance the Bamboula in Congo Square. "That was a sight to hold one rooted to the ground," Manna-Loulou says. "Mézor was as straight as a cypress-tree and as proud looking as a king. His body, bare to the waist, was like a column of ebony and it glistened like oil" (304). As Anna Shannon Elfenbein notes, "Zoraïde's love for Mézor, who is blacker than she, violates the racist notion that only white blood could beautify the African. Mézor is beautiful and princely, not in spite of his blackness, but because of it."[32]

Nevertheless, Madame Delarivière gasped, "That negro!" when she learned of the attraction, and she forbade Zoraïde to speak with Mézor. Yet, Manna-Loulou continues, "you know how the negroes are." "There is," she tells Madame Delisle, "no mistress, no master, no king nor priest who can hinder them from loving when they will. And these two found ways and means" (305). When Zoraïde became pregnant, Madame Delarivière had her friend sell Mézor, and when the baby was born, perfectly healthy, Madame Delarivière told Zoraïde the child was dead, hoping the beautiful slave would forget everything and return to being her devoted servant. Instead Zoraïde became insane, Manna-Loulou concludes, forever clutching a bundle of rags she imagined was her baby, rejecting her real child, already a toddler, when she is finally presented to her.

In "La Belle Zoraïde," Emily Toth writes, "Kate Chopin—the daughter of slave owners—looked on the thoughtless white world through the eyes of a woman of color, at a time when her Louisiana contemporaries Grace King and Ruth McEnery Stuart were still writing about happy slaves and tragic octoroons" (Toth, 222).

There is a parallel, as Patricia Hopkins Lattin and others have pointed out,[33] between the slave Manna-Loulou and her white mistress Madame Delisle (the teller of the tale and the listener) and Zoraïde and

Madame Delarivière (the participants in the narrative). Neither white woman is able to understand the position of her black slave. "Ah, the poor little one," Madame Delisle tells Manna-Loulou upon hearing Zoraïde's story, responding to the plight of the child but not that of the child's mother. "Better had she died!" (307).

Madame Delisle is no more able to identify with the position of Zoraïde or, apparently, her own servant, Manna-Loulou, than Armand Aubigny is able to imagine himself in the place of his wife, Désirée, and—judging by the picture of Madame Delisle that Chopin offers in "A Lady of Bayou St. John," the last story in *Bayou Folk*—for a similar reason.

Madame Delisle lives a fantasy that is childish more than childlike. She is ravished by her own beauty, "sitting for hours before the mirror, contemplating her own loveliness; admiring the brilliancy of her golden hair, the sweet languor of her blue eyes, the graceful contours of her figure, and the peach-like bloom of her flesh." Her husband has left to fight in the Civil War, but she is "not able to realize the significance of the tragedy whose unfolding kept the civilized world in suspense. It was only the immediate effect of the awful drama that moved her: the gloom that, spreading on all sides, penetrated her own existence and deprived it of joyousness" (298).

"The days and the nights were very lonely for Madame Delisle," the story begins (298), and, in her loneliness, she accepts the attention of a young French neighbor and agrees to run away to Paris with him. But the news arrives that her husband has been killed, and Madame Delisle at once begins the mourning she will continue throughout "the long years of widowhood" with "never a breath of reproach" (302).

The story could be called sentimental if it were read alone, outside its position in *Bayou Folk*. It could be accused of being excessively emotional, deficient in ethical judgment, of carrying characteristics common to the nineteenth-century popular domestic novel, like the phrasing that describes how the young French neighbor—who hopes to carry off Madame Delisle to Paris—struggles "in the fruitless mental effort of trying to comprehend that psychological enigma, a woman's heart" (302).

But reading all of *Bayou Folk* should make clear it is not "a woman's heart" Chopin is describing here, but *this* woman's, and this woman's as understood through the consciousness of a young romantic—himself, to some extent, a sentimentalist, though also, to some extent, another Chopin young person seeking to make the most of a bad situation, seeking what happiness he can eke out of the environment he finds himself in. As George Arms has written, even if Chopin "often falls into commercial sentimentalism, she refuses to be satisfied with this; she refuses to yield to the temptation of becoming a final interpreter out of her conviction that a realist may reveal most successfully that truth exists in a constant state of tension" (Arms, 226).

Most of the stories in *Bayou Folk* had appeared before—two in regional publications, most of the rest in *Vogue,* the *Century, Youth's Companion,* or *Harper's Young People,* magazines with impressive national circulations. Children's stories, those published in children's magazines or written for a children's audience, alternate in *Bayou Folk* with adult stories. Publications like *Youth's Companion* or *Harper's Young People* were understood as family magazines, and though they sought stories accessible to a juvenile audience, they had high editorial standards and were read by editors of adult magazines. Many nineteenth-century authors began their careers by writing for children.

Perhaps the inclusion of many children's stories helped make *Bayou Folk* Kate Chopin's most popular book for almost 80 years. The volume begins with a childlike burst of hope and sustains an optimistic character through many of its narratives. But it ends on a note of gloom that becomes stronger in Chopin's second book of short stories and dominates the third.

A Night in Acadie

A Night in Acadie (1897) is Kate Chopin's most balanced, most mature, most fully developed book of short stories. The characters in many of the 21 stories in the volume are older now and facing long-term dilemmas. Some continue to search for marriage partners, but others are questioning their marriages or their decisions not to marry, confronting the difficulties of their economic situations, or struggling with deep fears or prejudices. Only a third of the *Night in Acadie* stories, not half, as in *Bayou Folk*, were written for children.

Bayou Folk motifs, themes, and images appear in new forms in *A Night in Acadie* stories. Houses, outsiders, race, poverty, violence, sex, boundaries, and, as much as before, a search for balance are present over and over.

Chopin planned a third book of stories, *A Vocation and a Voice*, one not published during her lifetime, but she did not surpass the power of *A Night in Acadie*. The volume ranks with Washington Irving's *Sketch Book* (1820), Edgar Allan Poe's *Tales of the Grotesque and Arabesque* (1840), Nathaniel Hawthorne's *Mosses from an Old Manse* (1846), and Hamlin Garland's *Main-Travelled Roads* (1891) as one of America's great nineteenth-century anthologies of short stories.

"Ripe Figs" and "A Matter of Prejudice"

The tiny sketch "Ripe Figs" (1892), though positioned near the end of *A Night in Acadie*, is an ideal introduction to the volume:

> Maman-Nainaine said that when the figs were ripe Babette might go to visit her cousins down on the Bayou-Lafourche where the sugar cane grows. Not that the ripening of figs had the least thing to do with it, but that is the way Maman-Nainaine was.
>
> It seemed to Babette a very long time to wait; for the leaves upon the trees were tender yet, and the figs were like little hard, green marbles.

But warm rains came along and plenty of strong sunshine, and though Maman-Nainaine was as patient as the statue of la Madone, and Babette as restless as a humming-bird, the first thing they both knew it was hot summer-time. Every day Babette danced out to where the fig-trees were in a long line against the fence. She walked slowly beneath them, carefully peering between the gnarled, spreading branches. But each time she came disconsolate away again. What she saw there finally was something that made her sing and dance the whole long day.

When Maman-Nainaine sat down in her stately way to breakfast, the following morning, her muslin cap standing like a aureole about her white, placid face, Babette approached. She bore a dainty porcelain platter, which she set down before her godmother. It contained a dozen purple figs, fringed around with their rich, green leaves.

"Ah," said Maman-Nainaine, arching her eyebrows, "how early the figs have ripened this year!"

"Oh," said Babette, "I think they have ripened very late."

"Babette," continued Maman-Nainaine, as she peeled the very plumpest figs with her pointed silver fruit-knife, "you will carry my love to them all down on Bayou-Lafourche. And tell your Tante Frosine I shall look for her at Toussaint—when the chrysanthemums are in bloom." (199)

"Ripe Figs" sets out an important motif in *A Night in Acadie*, an emphasis on the way culture, Creole culture, shapes Creoles', 'Cajuns', blacks', and others' understanding of what is natural. With absolute ease Maman-Nainaine measures space and time through natural points of reference. When the figs are ripe, her goddaughter Babette may visit her cousins who live "where the sugar cane grows," and Babette's aunt will return the visit "at Toussaint—when the chrysanthemums are in bloom." Maman-Nainaine offers no explanation for her decrees: "Not that the ripening of figs had the least thing to do with it," the narrator notes, "but that is the way Maman-Nainaine was."

That is the way many people in Chopin's fiction are, people who speak and act with authority and who by their words and actions show others that the authority they possess is deserved, is just, intrinsic, as "natural" as the ease with which they live their lives and influence other people's.

Earlier in the volume, the touching little story "A Matter of Prejudice" (1893) illuminates the authority of a Maman-Nainaine through a portrait of a woman who mercilessly shuts her son and his family out of her life until she recognizes the price she pays for her actions and moves quickly and surely to remedy the matter. "Old Madame Carambeau," the narrator notes, "was a woman of many prejudices—so many, in fact, that it would be difficult to name them all. She detested dogs, cats, organ-grinders, white servants and children's noises. She despised Americans, Germans and all people of a different faith from her own. Anything not French had, in her opinion, little right to existence." The elderly widow finds the English language "hideous" and believes that "the Irish voice is distressing to the sick" (282–85). She has banished her son for 10 years because he married an American woman, and she has never entered the American quarter of New Orleans.

The houses in "A Matter of Prejudice" embody the values people carry or seek. Madame Carambeau's old Spanish mansion near the Mississippi River in the French quarter of New Orleans has "an impenetrable board fence, edged with a formidable row of iron spikes" which protects it from people—or foreign ideas—seeking entrance. Her son's "very modern and very handsome" home in the American quarter is, like the other houses in the district, open to the street—and by implication to other cultural influences—"not hidden behind spiked fences" (282, 87). The narrative is set in motion by the appearance of a sick child, Madame Carambeau's granddaughter, who needs the old woman's care and who, while being nursed back to health, breaks through the surface of her ancient prejudices.

Madame Carambeau transforms herself—she goes to Christmas mass at an American church and presents herself at her son's home to invite him and his family to dinner. But she does so with such ease and confidence, characteristics of the most prestigious members of the Creole community, that she maintains, even enhances, her position of dominance. At the mass she looks "as if she had been attending St. Patrick's church all her life. She sat with unruffled calm through the long service and through a lengthy English sermon, of which she did not understand a word." At her son's house, "not once did she show a sign of weakness; not even when her son, Henri, came and took her in his arms and sobbed and wept upon her neck as only a warm-hearted Creole could." And when she insists it was Providence, not an accident, that her grandchild should have become sick while attending a party at her house, "no one contradicted her" (286–87).

Everyone seems to believe that it is natural for Madame Carambeau to command. "You see," she tells her daughter-in-law at the close of the story, "I have no prejudices. I am not like my son. Henri was always a stubborn boy. Heaven only knows how he came by such a character!" (288). It is a telling sentence. Henri has inherited with his language and dispositions the confidence that give him the natural authority his mother has, that let him shape what those around him see as natural. His house may have a modern, open look about it, but what happens inside the building is an outgrowth of his mother's Creole confidence.

Also inside this bright little story—one published in a children's magazine—is an insightful treatment of the tensions that exist among successive generations of French settlers living in New Orleans in the 1870s. The story shows how a third-generation child impulsively jumps into the lap of an old woman, a first-generation immigrant, and reconciles the woman to what she sees as the treason of her son.

Madame Carambeau is an immigrant in spirit if not in fact. Chopin would have met many people of her age and disposition in the city. Comparatively large numbers of French immigrants had come to the United States in the 1840s and 1850s (few came during the Civil War), and again in the 1870s, and many settled in Louisiana.[34]

The old woman is what twentieth-century ethnic specialists like Marcus Lee Hansen or Werner Sollors call a "founder," a representative first-generation immigrant, true to the traditions she learned at home in France or in the enclaves of New Orleans where French culture is preserved.[35] There is nothing ironic about her singing "Partant pour la Syrie" ("Leaving for Syria"), a song of empire, celebrating Napoleon's advance into northern Africa, or about her holding a bottle of smelling salts to her nostrils when she drives for the first time into the American section of the city, even though the smell of roses is everywhere.

Her son Henri is a representative "traitor," a second-generation ethnic who marries an American, escapes from the French quarter of the city to the American, and forbids his daughter to speak French.

And Henri's daughter, the child who, by touching Madame Carambeau, reconciles the two older generations, is representative of a third or later generation of immigrants, a "redeemer." By returning to the mother tongue—Madame Carambeau will teach her French—the child will become what Sollors calls a "proper" ethnic, neither obsessive about nor indifferent to her ethnic tradition, neither ethnocentric nor assimilated, neither prejudiced against the new nor ignorant of the old (Sollors, 190). She will, like another third- or fourth-generation "redeemer," Kate Chopin herself, become bicultural, balanced, able to celebrate her ethnic background.

"A Respectable Woman"

Although the title of "A Respectable Woman" (1894) refers to Mrs. Baroda, the wife of planter Gaston Baroda, the narrative is propelled by a New Orleans journalist named Gouvernail, one of Chopin's most memorable characters. He has a major part in "Athénaïse" and he mutters an ominous warning at Edna Pontellier's housewarming party in *The Awakening*.[36] Gouvernail is the most sophisticated of Chopin's sensitive urban bachelors, men like Wallace Offdean of "A No-Account Creole" or Hector Santien of "In and Out of Old Natchitoches." Like Offdean, who means "to use his faculties intelligently" and to "keep clear of the maelstroms of sordid work and senseless pleasure," Gouvernail—something of a mature, literary Offdean—seeks balance in his life. He is visiting Gaston, his college friend, on his plantation this spring because he is "run down by overwork." "This is what I call living," he sighs as he sits on the portico smoking his cigar, listening to Gaston describe his experience as a sugar planter (334).

In "Athénaïse" Chopin presents what is happening in the narrative partly through Gouvernail's consciousness. Here she presents Gouvernail through the consciousness of Mrs. Baroda, who, without being aware of it, seeks something more than what her life offers her. She and her husband "had entertained a good deal during the winter; much of the time had also been passed in New Orleans in various forms of mild dissipation. She was looking forward to a period of unbroken rest, now, and undisturbed tête-à-tête with her husband" (333). She is not happy when her husband invites Gouvernail—whom she has never met—to visit and is convinced that she will not like him. He is not a society man, she reasons, and he is a journalist, so he is probably cynical and probably wears eyeglasses.

Yet though he does not seek her company and puts forth no effort to make her like him, Mrs. Baroda finds him a "lovable, inoffensive fellow" (334). He is physically attractive, and, as Allen F. Stein points out, by his very nature, he "calls her own way of life into question," he forces her to examine "just how powerful her underlying need to scrutinize her life has been."[37]

Gouvernail apparently understands Mrs. Baroda's position perfectly well. Sitting alongside her in the dark, he quotes aloud lines from Walt Whitman's "Song of Myself": "Night of south winds—night of the large few stars! / Still nodding night—" (335).[38]

Mrs. Baroda does not reply, but Gouvernail begins to talk "freely and intimately in a low, hesitating drawl" about "old college days . . . of keen and blind ambitions and large intentions" and about how he is left with "a philosophic acquiescence to the existing order—only a desire to be permitted to exist, with now and then a little whiff of genuine life, such as he was breathing now." Mrs. Baroda's "physical being" becomes "predominant": "She wanted to reach out her hand in the darkness and touch him with the sensitive tips of her fingers upon the face or the lips. She wanted to draw close to him and whisper against his cheek—she did not care what—as she might have done if she had not been a respectable woman" (335).

When she leaves, Gouvernail ends his "apostrophe to the night" from Whitman (336), which Chopin does not include for her readers but which reads, "Press close bare-bosomed night—press close magnetic nourishing night! / Night of south winds—night of the large few stars! / Still nodding night—mad naked summer night."

The narrative stays focused throughout on the consciousness of Mrs. Baroda. She escapes her feelings by telling her husband that she does not like his friend and that she must make a shopping trip to New Orleans until after Gouvernail leaves, and she objects to her husband's plans to have him return in the summer.

And then Kate Chopin, who orchestrates endings as well as any American ever has, describes Mrs. Baroda's temptation to share her feelings with her husband, her realization that "there are some battles in life which a human being must fight alone," and her proposal, near the end of the year, to invite Gouvernail back. When Gaston tells her he is glad she has "overcome" her dislike for Gouvernail, she responds by giving him "a long, tender kiss upon his lips" and saying, "I have overcome everything! you will see. This time I shall be very nice to him" (336).

Whatever it is Mrs. Baroda means by those words, Gouvernail's visit has revealed to her options she had not much examined before.

"Athénaïse"

"Athénaïse" (1895) is Kate Chopin's richest short story, a nineteenth-century classic. It shares with "A Respectable Woman" the central presence of the sophisticated journalist Gouvernail and with *The Awakening* its structure shaped by a pregnancy. It is a tour de force of some of Chopin's major motifs and themes—going away and coming back, the presence of an outsider, the cultural construction of the natural. It is Chopin's most complex exploration of a person's instinctual reach for a life of abundant personal and social possibilities.

Its opening and closing reveal its fundamental direction. On the first page, Athénaïse Miché is rebellious child, running from her husband of two months to her parents, raging about how she cannot be happy in her own way, focused on her frustration, confusion, and misery. On the last page, she is ecstatic adult, clinging to her husband, delighted with nature, other people, and herself, focused on the child she is carrying within her.

The story is balanced between five sections set on the rigolet de Bon Dieu where Athénaïse grew up and where she met Cazeau, the widower she chose to marry, and six longer sections set in New Orleans where she arrives at some perspective, sifts through her options, intuitively finds herself. It is permeated with a sense of ambiguity.

"Athénaïse" has not been a favorite with some critics because of what they see as a disappointing ending in which a strong, vibrant woman desperately seeking a better existence settles for the ordinary satisfactions of motherhood and life with a domineering husband. But the story is consistent with the vision of life embodied in most of Chopin's best work. Athénaïse sacrifices some of what a modern reader might see as the possibilities of an urban life in New Orleans, but those are not possibilities Athénaïse considers for herself. And everyone in the story, not just Athénaïse, makes sacrifices—certainly Cazeau, Athénaïse's husband, and Monteclin, her brother, and Gouvernail, the journalist who becomes enchanted with Athénaïse during her month in New Orleans.

Just how little people's decisions appear as reasoned or rational in Chopin's works is set forth brilliantly in "Athénaïse." In *The Awakening,* Edna Pontellier is pictured as having "apprehended instinctively the dual life—that outward existence which conforms, the inward life which questions" (893) and as "blindly following whatever impulse moved her, as if she had placed herself in alien hands for direction, and freed her soul of responsibility" (913). Athénaïse is younger than Edna, less experienced, much less conscious of what is happening to her. She knows only that she hates being married and is repelled by sex. "I can't stan' to live with a man," she tells her brother, "to have him always there; his coats an' pantaloons hanging in my room; his ugly bare feet— washing them in my tub, befo' my very eyes, ugh!" (431).

Chopin uses the image of bare feet at several places in her works to generate an aura of sexuality. Edna Pontellier in *The Awakening* notices that Mariequita, a Spanish woman with uncertain connections to both Robert Lebrun and his brother Victor, has sand and slime between her toes. Suzima in "A Vocation and a Voice" attracts the boy in the story to her by lying down in a moving wagon and letting her bare feet stick out over the edge so that the boy, who is walking behind the cart and who has recently seen her sitting naked washing those feet in a pool of water, comes to her.

Athénaïse feels lost, unable to cope with marriage, because she has "an instinctive realization of the futility of rebellion against a social and sacred institution" (432). She does not see where to turn, what to turn toward: "People often said that Athénaïse would know her own mind some day, which was equivalent to saying that she was at present unacquainted with it. If she ever came to such knowledge, it would be by no intellectual research, by no subtle analyses or tracing the motives of actions to their source. It would come to her as the song to the bird, the perfume and color to the flower" (433).

Athénaïse does not understand why she chose Cazeau as her husband. In part, she thinks, it was because girls married when the chance came, but also because Cazeau would "make life more comfortable for her" and because "she had liked him, and had even been rather flustered when he pressed her hands and kissed them, and kissed her lips and cheeks and eyes, when she accepted him" (430).

If Athénaïse acts because of socialized dispositions deeper than conscious thought, so does her husband, Cazeau. "I married you," he tells her when she pathetically demands some explanation for her misery and the wretched state of their marriage, "because I loved you; because you were the woman I wanted to marry, an' the only one. . . . I did think that I might make you happy in making things easier an' mo' comfortable fo' you. . . . I believed that yo' coming yere to me would be like the sun shining out of the clouds" (435).

His sense of hopelessness is as profound as hers. When he brings her back from her parents early in the story, he is reminded of his father's returning a runaway slave, and a "humiliating sensation of baseness" overcomes him, a "terrible sense of loss," a "realization of having missed a chance for happiness,—a chance that would come his way again only through a miracle." And he is especially pained when Athénaïse leaves a second time, at night, secretly, because he believes he has not thrust himself upon her. He had lived alone as a widower for 10 years, rejecting women who pursued him, until Athénaïse appeared and attracted him, he remembers, "with eyes, with voice, with a hundred womanly ways, and finally distracted him with love which she seemed, in her timid, maidenly fashion, to return" (438–39). Cazeau has what Barbara Ewell calls a "blunt integrity" (Ewell, 112).

Even Gouvernail, the journalist Athénaïse meets during her month in New Orleans, follows the promptings of his dispositions—though ironically he is as fully conscious a person as exists in Chopin's fiction, the individual who comes closest to putting into language a vision of life that Chopin communicates implicitly in her stories. In other works, Gouvernail gives form to his insights by quoting fragments of poetry that reveal their intentions only to readers who can reconstruct their context—in "A Respectable Woman" a piece of Walt Whitman's "Song of Myself," in *The Awakening* a sonnet of Algernon Swinburne. In "Athénaïse" he is aware that the charming, beautiful, but vulnerable woman living in the next room in his boardinghouse cannot be offered the kind of poetry he reads and apparently discusses with his circle of "advanced" thinkers in the American quarter of the city (444). Athénaïse has poured out her heart to him, and he understands that she adores her brother Montéclin and suspects that she adores Cazeau without knowing it. He sees that she is "self-willed, impulsive, innocent, ignorant, unsatisfied, dissatisfied" (446).

All three men in the intimate circle around Athénaïse yield to her instincts, adjust their own needs to hers. Her brother Montéclin will do whatever Athénaïse asks of him, in part because he loves her, in part because he hates her husband, who has refused to loan him money. He secretly whisks her away to New Orleans, borrows money to keep her there, and brings her back to Cazeau when she asks, though he—like some modern critics—is disappointed that she ends up behaving in such an "ordinary" manner (454). Cazeau writes to her, telling her that she is free not to come back to him "unless she came of her free will . . . unless she could be the companion he had hoped for in marrying her, and in some measure return affection and respect for the love which he continued and would always continue to feel for her" (439). And Gouvernail, with Athénaïse crying in his arms, struggles to control himself:

> He understood a thousand times better than she herself understood it that he was acting as substitute for Montéclin. Bitter as the conviction was, he accepted it. He was patient; he could wait. He hoped some day to hold her with a lover's arms. That she was married made no particle of difference to Gouvernail. He could not conceive or dream of it making a difference. When the time came that she wanted him,—as he hoped and believed it would come,—he felt he would have a right to her. So long as she did not want him, he had no right to her,—no more than her husband had. (450)

Yet it is not to a man that Athénaïse responds. It is to the new life within her, the recognition of which shakes her to the core. Now when she thinks of Cazeau, "the first purely sensuous tremor of her life swept over her." She whispers his name, "and the sound of it brought red blotches into her cheeks. She spoke it over and over, as if it were some new, sweet sound born out of darkness and confusion, and reaching her for the first time. . . . Her whole passionate nature was aroused as if by a miracle." The letter she sends to Cazeau she writes "with a single thought, a spontaneous impulse," and when she asks for money from her husband's merchants (at the brokerage house where Wallace Offdean in "A No-Account Creole" works), she does so with "an air of partnership, almost proprietorship" (451–52) because she reaches for the life that will be most fulfilling for her, the life that offers her the greatest rewards, that she participates in as partner, coproprietor.

No one understands what she is doing so well as Gouvernail. He sees that she has forgotten him, learns why from their landlady, in whom Athénaïse has confided, and is kind to her, helping her get on her way back to her husband. He has lost, he recognizes. Athénaïse has chosen the better life. "He was a man of intelligence, and took defeat gracefully; that was all. But as he made his way back to the carriage, he was thinking, 'By heaven, it hurts, it hurts!' " (453).

"Tante Cat'rinette"

Like "Beyond the Bayou," one of Chopin's children's stories, "Tante Cat'rinette" (1894) tells of a free black woman who responds to a need of her former master's family by breaking out of her fears to cross a boundary she has constructed and studiously maintained.

The narrative emphasizes the woman's membership in a community. "It happened just as every one had predicted," the story begins, showing us first what the community sees, "Tante Cat'rinette was beside herself with rage and indignation when she learned that the town authorities had . . . condemned her house and intended to demolish it" because parts were so dilapidated they threatened the safety of people passing by (337). "Every one" in Natchitoches understands the importance of that house—a building again is a central image in this story—as an emblem of Cat'rinette's freedom and security, given to her by Vieumaite, her "old master," because 35 years earlier her careful nursing had saved the life of his daughter after the doctors said the child would die. And the people of the town, including Lawyer Paxton (who in *Bayou Folk* hopes to marry Madame Célestin), follow with interest Cat'rinette's determination to hold on to the house even if she must wield her ax to protect it. The local children terrorize her, singing beneath her windows: "Tante Cat'rinette, she go to town; / W'en she come back, her house pull' down" (338). So Cat'rinette will not leave the house.

But the old woman accepts the continuing authority of Vieumaite, whom she has come to imagine as inhabiting a region of splendor "up there overhead where the sun and stars and moon are" (343). When she learns that the 35-year-old Miss Kitty—Vieumaite had named the child "Cat'rine" after her—is sick and that she and her husband cannot afford a servant or a doctor, Cat'rinette visits the couple. She travels secretly at night so no one will know she has left the town. Returning home through the forest, frightened about her house, worried about Miss Kitty, conscious of the animals about her, and thinking of Vieumaite, the sudden appearance of the dawn seems to startle her and at the same time to comfort her with its beauty and peacefulness:

> Across the narrow, quivering line of water, the delicate budding branches of young trees were limned black against the gold, orange,— what word is there to tell the color of that morning sky! And steeped in the splendor of it hung one pale star; there was not another in the whole heaven.
>
> Tante Cat'rinette stood with her eyes fixed intently upon that star, which held her like a hypnotic spell. She stammered breathlessly:
>
> "Mo pé couté, Vieumaite. Cat'rinette pé couté." (I am listening, Vieumaite. Cat'rinette hears you.)
>
> She stayed there motionless upon the brink of the river till the star melted into the brightness of the day and became part of it. (343)

Her decision to sell her house to the town, to loan Miss Kitty and her husband the $1,000 the authorities have offered her for the building, and to move in with the dispossessed Kitty comes not from her own initiative, she insists, but from her master in heaven: "It's Vieumaite tell me all dat clair an' plain dis mo'nin'," she says (344). By rejoining the family whom she loves and who loves her, Cat'rinette transforms her social relationship with them. By helping them in their need, she helps herself as well. She will no longer be a prisoner in her own house, no longer alienated from her community.

"Nég Créol"

Chopin published three stories in the *Atlantic Monthly:* "Tante Cat'rinette," "Athénaïse," and "Nég Créol" (1896). The third has been ignored by most critics. It may seem on first reading no more than a character sketch of a pathetic eccentric, like something out of Guy de Maupassant, a rehearsal for a story, rather than a story in itself. And because Chicot, the old black nég créol—oppressed, poverty-stricken, and ignorant—is fiercely loyal to the white Boisduré family, whom he served before the Civil War, the story may seem to reinforce a hateful racial stereotype.

Yet "Nég Créol" is a brilliantly conceived picture of a helpless, dominated person building an identity for himself by secret loving attention to someone even worse off than he is and by continuous public defense of his once glorious association with a noble white family, which, he says, maintains its splendor today.

Old Chicot is presented to us through the consciousness of the itinerant merchants of the teeming, clamorous, multicultural French market in New Orleans—the "Dagoes" who "squealed like rats," the Gascon butchers who "bellowed like bulls," the "Hebrews," Choctaws, Irish, Sicilians, mulattoes, blacks, and others. It is within that consciousness that he seeks to preserve and enhance his identity. He preaches to the merchants about the Boisduré glory he knows was true decades ago and that he insists is—or, he believes, should be—true today (506).

His name is César François Xavier but the people in the market call him "Nég" or "Maringouin" (insect, mosquito) or "Chicot" (stump) because he is "so black, lean, lame, and shriveled." He not only accepts the names people give him but is convinced his very existence is a direct product of a community effort, that he was created not by God, "Michié bon Dieu," but by two members of the first Christian community, the apostles "Michié St. Pierre et Michié St. Paul," because that is what his former master, "a lax believer, and a great *farceur*," had told him. And he accepts without question the glory of his former master Jean Boisduré, who, he believes, has left behind "a progeny, rich, cultured, powerful, and numerous. . . . men of note and position, whose names were familiar to the public. . . . ladies who came to the market in carriages, or whose elegance of attire attracted the attention and admiration of the fish-women." Although he does not seek recognition by them, he talks constantly about "their dignity and pride of birth and wealth" (505–6).

If consistency of character is, as Irving Howe argues, a hallmark of good fiction, if memorable characters have "something awesome, even a little frightening about them since, for all their vividness of being, what finally matters most about them is their destiny,"[39] then Chicot sticks in a reader's mind because at one of the great defining moments of his life, he remains true to his deepest instincts.

No one at the French market knows that Chicot lives only to serve the desperately poor, 75-year-old Aglaé Boisduré, that he gathers each day whatever he earns for cleaning the stalls of the merchants—a handkerchief, a bottle of *filé*, a soup bone, some crabs or shrimps—and brings them to her in her apartment high in the top floor of an old building where he patiently hears her complaints about her health and her neighbors (though not about her poverty, which Chicot considers a "disgrace") before retreating to spend the night in his tarred paper chicken coop on Bayou St. John (the bayou along which Manna-Loulou in *Bayou Folk* tells Madame Delisle about La Belle Zoraïde). Chicot would gladly give up his life to help Aglaé Boisduré, but when the old woman dies, when his last link to his master is broken, he responds by being true to the family's former glory, not their later decline. He refuses to recognize Aglaé's funeral procession as it passes by the French market, insisting that all the Boisdurés descended from his master are wealthy.

A sense of irony infuses the scene as the last Boisduré (the word means "durable wood") is rolled with apparently little notice through the streets of the vibrantly alive market, past the stalls run by Italians and Irish and Jews. The vitality is gone from the once proud family, and their memory is in the hands of a nég créol, who turns away from the procession and goes on scaling his red snapper. Yet "this portrait," as Barbara Ewell calls it, "of the struggle for self-respect among the poor" (Ewell, 122) is a delicate treatment of how at least one African American seeks to make a life for himself amid the economic collapse that accompanied the end of the Civil War.

Chopin's Treatment of Race

Kate Chopin was a nineteenth-century Southerner. Her family owned slaves while she was growing up in St. Louis. Her husband was a member of the notorious White League, a group of armed Democrats that in 1874 clashed so violently with Republican Radicals that President Grant sent in federal troops.

In stories like "Nég Créol," "Tante Cat'rinette," "La Belle Zoraïde" "Beyond the Bayou," "Désirée's Baby," and others, Chopin explores with sensitivity the painful, desperate position of African Americans in the South both before and after the Civil War and documents some tragic results of whites' attitudes toward race. In other stories—"Mamouche," "Odalie Misses Mass," "The Lilies," and others—Chopin's descriptions of stereotypical "darkies" may be unsettling and disturbing for modern readers. They seem uncharacteristic of a person so aware of cultural differences and so committed to individual freedom.

Scholars have for many years been examining Kate Chopin's attitude toward race and have sought to understand how Chopin views the position of black people. Their opinions vary, and their discussions raise some complex questions.

Barbara Ewell argues that Chopin, being a product of her society, must have interiorized common Southern white attitudes toward race. She "never quite overcame her racial biases," Ewell says, and she carries an "ambivalence about race" (Ewell, 67, 72).

Per Seyersted, who edited Chopin's *Complete Works* and wrote the first modern Chopin biography, concludes that African Americans in Chopin's works sometimes appear as stereotypes but that Chopin accepted black people "as persons worthy of serious study" and "treats them as people and with little condescension" (Seyersted, 79).

Anna Shannon Elfenbein notes that "the racial scene in Chopin's Natchitoches Parish was complex and might have taxed the powers of the most sociologically minded writer of fiction. However, Chopin was unusually nonchalant about observing racial distinctions that were crucial to her Cane River neighbors but less significant to a woman with a St. Louis origin." Chopin, Elfenbein notes, "exploits the blurred racial categories of the milieu she describes. Because her treatment of race and ethnicity is sometimes negligent and sometimes purposeful, many readers have been baffled by those stories that present the complex and ambiguous racial categories of nineteenth-century Louisiana" (Elfenbein, 120).

Daniel Aaron writes, "If she had a patriarchal attitude toward the 'darky's,' as she often referred to them, and relied heavily on the 'faithful retainer' stereotype, the blacks were not invisible or conglomerate. She looked at them and listened to them attentively and empathetically." Kate Chopin, he continues, "engaged in no public controversies. She carried on a private civil war between contending principles in her own nature, and I wonder if it isn't this contest that accounts for the tensions in her best stories" (Aaron, 347).

Helen Taylor considers Kate Chopin "politically conservative and—to a modern sensibility—deeply racist."[40] "Although Chopin's works and personal writings point to a considerable critical engagement in questions of gender and the position of women," she argues in *Gender, Race, and Region in the Writings of Grace King, Ruth McEnery Stuart, and Kate Chopin,* "they indicate no such involvement in the problems of race and southern blacks."

> When one examines the work for complex treatments of race, what emerges is a sentimental and anodyne view of Louisiana blacks and mulattoes, one that confirms their simplicity, fidelity to and love for whites, and constructs them as cheery figures acting out a pastoral subplot to the comic or tragic dramas of white communities. . . . Her short stories and sketches, set mainly in Louisiana's Cane River area, had to ignore the historical realities of extreme poverty and racial violence, its anachronistic plantation economy, and the tensions between poor whites and freedmen/women, and landowning whites and free mulattoes. And she used the dialect of her subordinate black figures . . . to patronize and amuse. (Taylor, 156–57)[41]

Richard H. Potter describes four black people in Chopin's short stories—Pa-Jeff of "A Dresden Lady in Dixie," Chicot of "Nég Créol," Aunt Pinky of "Odalie Misses Mass," and Tante Cat'rinette. All are former slaves, yet, Potter argues, Chopin gives them "distinct personalities":

> She shows us how they were affected by slavery by probing the psychological implications of slavery in their individual lives. Each character reacts differently despite the mutuality of experience. Each character's story is a separate and individual study of the particular way he or she is affected by a particular past. Thus, while all were slaves, they are still distinct human beings with unique and individual lives.
>
> What is most significant about her is not that she can be labeled liberal or traditional in terms of modern polarizations. For Mrs. Chopin observed rather than instructed, demonstrated rather than judged. And she observed many blacks who were proud, individualistic human beings. Especially with those to whom she gave the greatest care and delineations she went beyond race and found humanity. (Potter, 55, 58)

And Emily Toth, who has written the most detailed Chopin biography to date, notes that "Chopin's description of black people—jarring to current sensibilities—would have been considered liberal in her day" (Toth, 269) and adds that in her work Chopin "never depicts social

45

equality between blacks and whites, but such equality existed rarely, if at all, in real life. . . . As a writer, Kate Chopin was not interested in men's political battles over race, but she portrayed black women, especially mothers, with sympathy and deep feeling" (Toth, 136).

Discussions about Kate Chopin's treatment of race raise important questions about how readers today are to sort out for themselves attitudes toward race in American writers living before recent decades. One careful discussion of the subject comes from Toni Morrison in the preface to *Playing in the Dark: Whiteness and the Literary Imagination:*

> For reasons that should not need explanation here, until very recently, and regardless of the race of the author, the readers of virtually all of American fiction have been positioned as white. I am interested to know what that assumption has meant to the literary imagination. When does racial "unconsciousness" or awareness of race enrich interpretive language, and when does it impoverish it? What does positing one's writerly self, in the wholly racialized society that is the United States, as unraced and all others as raced entail? . . . Living in a nation of people who *decided* that their world view would combine agendas for individual freedom *and* mechanisms for devastating racial oppression presents a singular landscape for a writer. When this world view is taken seriously as agency, the literature produced within and without it offers an unprecedented opportunity to comprehend the resilience and gravity, the inadequacy and the force of the imaginative act.
>
> Thinking about these matters has challenged me as a writer and a reader. It has made both activities harder and infinitely more rewarding. It has, in fact, elevated and sharpened the delight I take in the work that literature, under the pressure that racialized societies level on the creative process, manages to do. Over and over again I am amazed by the treasure trove that American literature is. How compelling is the study of those writers who take responsibility for *all* of the values they bring to their art. How stunning is the achievement of those who have searched for and mined a shareable language for the words to say it.[42]

Kate Chopin was a product of the culture she grew up in and spent her life within—nineteenth-century culture, American culture, Southern culture—so she interiorized attitudes toward African Americans carried by what Morrison calls a "wholly racialized" way of life. It would be foolish to argue otherwise.

But as this volume has emphasized, Chopin lived also within French culture; she struggled to find balance between and among the values she carried, and she gives form to that struggle in her stories—examining one idea here, one question there, looking in one work at what life is like and imagining in another what it could be like if things were different. She reaches throughout her fiction for something that she never quite completely grasps.

Her often agonized search for truth focuses at times on gender or culture, at times on race. Some of her stories about blacks do little more than reflect Southern attitudes in the 1890s. But some—"Nég Créol," "Tante Cat'rinette," "La Belle Zoraïde," "Beyond the Bayou," "Désirée's Baby," and a few others—do much more. They capture the pain and desperateness but also the richness and complexity of the lives of individual African Americans forcefully, eloquently, beautifully. They are a treasure for readers today.

"Regret," "At Chênière Caminada," and "A Sentimental Soul"

"Nég Créol" is the most intense of stories in *A Night in Acadie* that tell of people whose choices leave them in some way diminished, either because the object of their desire, like Chicot's beloved family, has vanished or because that object leads them away from an active involvement with daily life toward a concentration on death.

Mamzelle Aurélie in "Regret" (1894) is crying "with sobs that seemed to tear her very soul" at the end of her narrative because at age 50 she has discovered she blundered in having refused the possibility of marriage and a family (378).[43] The narrative details the conditions that brought about her discovery. Until her neighbor one morning drops four small children on her doorstep after the sudden illness of a parent, she has never thought about children, has been content with the running of her plantation and the presence of her dog, her field hands, her gun, and her religion. At first she approaches her new responsibilities as an unwanted duty and tells her cook, "Me, I'd rather manage a dozen plantation' than fo' chil'ren. It's terrassent! Bonté! Don't talk to me about chil'ren!" But after two weeks, she has become accustomed to "the laughing, the crying, the chattering that echoed through the house and around it all day long" and to sleeping "with little Elodie's hot, plump body pressed close against her, and the little one's warm breath beating her cheek like the fanning of a bird's wing" (377).

If Chicot has an awareness of having contributed in any way to the loss of his former glorious associations with the Boisdurés, we do not hear of it, but Mamzelle Aurélie cannot escape her own responsibility for her newly discovered emptiness. She had "never thought" of marrying and had "promptly declined" the proposal she had received, choosing to turn away from motherhood toward a man's life. Chopin surrounds her with male imagery; she wears a "man's hat" and an "old blue army overcoat," she carries a "gun (with which she shot chicken-hawks)" (375), and at the end of the story she cries "like a man" (378). She has through determination and hard work maintained the plantation life that Chicot cannot get back to, but she has forfeited a central part of what she now believes makes that life worth reaching for.

"At Chênière Caminada" (1893) vibrates with the music of *The Awakening*—sharing with the novel many of its settings, several of its characters, and some of its imagery.[44]

Chênière Caminada is off the coast of Louisiana, across Caminada Bay from Grand Isle. Like the novel, this short story shifts its setting from the coastal region to New Orleans and back. Madame Lebrun, who owns the pension on Grand Isle where Edna Pontellier and her family spend their summer, has a part to play in this story, as does Baptiste Beaudelet, who transports Edna in his lugger from Grand Isle to the Chênière, and Claire Duvigné, in whose presence Robert Lebrun had passed two summers sometime before Edna arrived on Grand Isle. The story is focused on Tonie Bocaze, the son of Madame Antoine, in whose cottage Edna falls asleep after she becomes sick at mass on the Chênière.

Like Chopin's novel, "At Chênière Caminada" is bathed in imagery of the sea, and like *The Awakening*, it presents the ocean as a place of "rest and peace" but also of death (316). Tonie Bocaze sees the ocean much as Edna Pontellier sees it. Edna, on first learning to swim, wants "to swim far out, where no woman had swum before" (908). Tonie wants to "go far, far out where the sound of no bell could reach him" (315). Edna ultimately drowns herself in the sea. Tonie does not, but only, apparently, because circumstances prevent him.

He had walked into church one Sunday morning and heard a joyous burst of organ music that threw him into deep confusion and changed his life. The church—the same one Edna Pontellier visits—is on the Chênière, and the music was being played by Claire Duvigné from New Orleans, a visitor on Grand Isle. Tonie had fallen instantly in love with the musical daughter of the famous New Orleans lawyer, but he has understood that his painful shyness, his "clumsy," "awkward" ways, and his simple Acadian life make him an impossible candidate for the young

Creole woman's love. When he is alone with her in his boat one afternoon, the "savage instinct of his blood" has urged him to clasp her in his arms and spring with her into the sea (314). He has resisted his instinct but learned a few months later that Claire has died from a chill.

The news has stunned Tonie, but over a period of months he has concluded that he is glad she is dead, because, he explains to his mother,

> "While she lived I could never hope for anything. . . . Despair was the only thing for me. There were always men about her. . . .
>
> "Oh, I could see her married to one of them—his wife—coming year after year to Grand Isle and bringing her little children with her! I can't tell you all that I saw—all that was driving me mad! But now . . . she is where she belongs; there is no difference up there; the curé has often told us there is no difference between men. It is with the soul that we approach each other there. Then she will know who has loved her best. That is why I am so contented. Who knows what may happen up there?" (318)

Chopin might have described this story as "mad," the word she uses to characterize some of the Maupassant stories she translated.

Mamzelle Fleurette in "A Sentimental Soul" (1894) has her heart set on a person as unattainable for her as Claire Duvigné is for Tonie Bocaze, and, like Tonie, she feels free to express her affection for her beloved only after his death. But the impulse for Fleurette's actions is quite different from that which drives Tonie's, suggesting a future quite the opposite for her.

Toni will live now for the afterlife. His hope is in the teachings of his priest, in submission to what he understands as religious faith. Fleurette, however, breaks with her priest after she confesses to him that she has fallen in love with a radical locksmith named Lacodi, a married man. Though there is in her "withered" face "little force or character or anything . . . except a pathetic desire and appeal to be permitted to exist" and though her love for Lacodie changes her world, making it "brighter and more beautiful" with flowers that "redoubled their sweetness" and with "voices of her fellow-creatures" that have become "kinder and their faces truer," the priest at the cathedral scolds her. He calls her a fool and a "sentimentalist" and orders her to stay away from Lacodie (389, 91).

Fleurette understands well enough that there is not likely any future for her with Lacodie—even were he not married, she is much older and taller than him—and she understands that she has neither his moral strength nor practical courage: "she held a vague understanding that men were wickeder in many ways than women; that ungodliness was constitutional with them, like their sex, and inseparable from it" (389). When Lacodie dies from a fever, she tries to forget him. Her priest has told her she must: "she did not question his authority, or his ability to master the subtleties of a situation utterly beyond reach of her own powers" (394).

But when Lacodie's widow remarries less than a year after the locksmith's death, Fleurette undergoes a "terrible upheaval." She finds a confessor in another church, does not tell him of her passion for Lacodie, and hangs a picture of a man who looks like her beloved between the "crucifix and the portrait of Empress Eugènie." She does not care if his widow ever sees it. She has by her lights become as radical as the blacksmith himself. She feels like she is "walking on air" and prepares "for the first time in her life to take her conscience into her own keeping" (396–97).

"After the Winter"

"After the Winter" (1891) is a "Nég Créol" in reverse, a portrait of an isolated man who, devastated by the loss of family, protects himself by adamantly concealing his private life—but M'sieur Michel is a wealthy white planter, not a poverty-stricken black stall cleaner, his loss is caused by a deep personal hurt, not a general economic collapse, so his way back to some semblance of plantation life is comparatively open rather than essentially closed. "After the Winter" is one of Chopin's most hopeful stories of *re*possession. And like a later story, "A Morning Walk," it is tied to a Christian perception of fulfillment through a communal celebration of rebirth.

Its three-part structure traces M'sieur Michel's movement from rejection of any need for "human sympathy and companionship" (186), through a period of restless doubt, to an eventual, tentative acceptance of reintegration into the community. Like Tante Cat'rinette and the nég créol, M'sieur Michel is introduced through the eyes of the group. Some of the younger members know no more about the life of M'sieur Michel than the people in the French market know of Chicot. They believe, however, that during his 25 years in "the hills" he has killed "two Choctaws, as many Texans, a free mulatto and numberless blacks"—a belief that older people know to be false but do not bother to correct (a belief, however, that underscores an awareness of violence below the surface of life in Chopin's stories). So they let him alone in the primitive cabin he built for himself when he returned from the Civil War to find his children dead and his wife gone off with someone else (181).

The narrative is played out over the Easter weekend. M'sieur Michel himself—the story eases into his consciousness—finds he has "nothing in common" with the people who live nearby or with their Easter "mummery." He harbors a "sentiment toward man, keener than indifference, bitter as hate" and dreads even the most elemental contact with people. Only when some children invade his woods to collect wildflowers for a church altar does he resolve to confront his neighbors, but he is startled when he arrives at the Easter morning service to have an "indignant mulatto" tell him, "Take off yo' hat!" (184–85), and even more startled to find himself obeying the command and withdrawing in confusion from the group's expressions of joy and peace. It is, however, a single person, not the community, who helps him break out of his pain and anger. When he approaches the plantation he abandoned 25 years earlier, he finds that it has not reverted to woodland as he had expected, that his neighbor, Joe Duplan, has maintained it for him, that it is ready to be occupied again.

Joe Duplan owns "Les Chêniers," where Euphraise Manton of "A No-Account Creole" grew up. Euphraise (she appears for just a moment in "After the Winter") comes to love the richness of her life at "Les Chêniers" and, apparently, to marry a man who will join her in creating something similar on another nearby plantation. M'sieur Michel, it seems, may regain his place in the community as well.

"A Night in Acadie"

The title story (and first story) in *A Night in Acadie* functions much like "A No-Account Creole" or "At the 'Cadian Ball" in *Bayou Folk*—locking in place themes and motifs of other stories.

The setting of "A Night in Acadie" (1896), repeating the "'Cadian Ball" motif in *Bayou Folk*, is a dance, a place where young people in the Acadian community can try out their options—make their best showing, dance their best steps, form and re-form their alliances in the surrounding darkness. The narrative is straightforward. An outsider arrives, offering by his presence a more attractive alternative to a woman who has already committed to someone else. Through physical force, through a violent confrontation, the outsider prevails.

The woman, Zaïda Trodon, is an Athénaïse Miché without good instincts, a 'Tite Reine (from "In Sabine" in *Bayou Folk*) who by sheer luck escapes a disastrous marriage. The outsider, 28-year-old Telèsphore Baquette, is neither cosmopolitan nor philosophical—neither a Wallace Offdean nor a Gouvernail—and he does not have clearly formulated what he wants out of life, defining himself mostly in terms of his uncle, after whom he is named. His uncle is illiterate, so Telèsphore learns to read and write; his uncle hunts, so Telèsphore does not; his uncle tells time by the sun, so Telèsphore always carries a watch. By "advisedly shaping his course in direct opposition to that of his uncle," Telèsphore manages to lead "a rather orderly, industrious, and respectable existence" (485).

Telèsphore does know that he wants a wife, yet he has difficulty choosing among the local women, not because they are unattractive but because each has something—eyes, skin, energy, charms, accomplishments, seductiveness, property—but none has everything. When he meets Zaïda on a train heading for Marksville in Avoyelles Parish (Chopin likes moving trains as places for social contacts, though sometimes people in her stories—Mrs. Baroda of "A Respectable Woman," Suzanne of "In and Out of Old Natchitoches," or Athénaïse—use a train to escape from an uncomfortable relationship), he sets his heart on her in part because in her presence he forgets what he was looking for. When he learns she is on her way to a ball, he resolves to join her.

The grinding poverty in Chopin's fiction is evident here in the house, which is "big, bulky and weather-beaten" and made up "chiefly of galleries in every stage of decrepitude and dilapidation" (490). Zaïda is the cousin of Mentine Trodon, the "piteously thin," "sadly misshapen" woman with four children whom Doudouce visits in "A Visit to Avoyelles" (229). Zaïda's wedding outfit is all white, even her slippers, but "no one would have believed let alone suspected that they were a pair of old black ones which she had covered with pieces of her first communion sash" (490–91).

Telèsphore is only marginally better off than Zaïda, so her poverty does not concern him. He is taken by her whole person, and Chopin's description of Telèsphore's reaction to Zaïda's beauty suggests phrasing in "The Storm": "How Zaïda's eyes sparkled now! What very pretty teeth Zaïda had when she laughed, and what a mouth! Her lips were a revelation, a promise; something to carry away and remember in the night and grow hungry thinking of next day" (491).

But Zaïda has promised to elope with André Pascal—unemployed, arrogant, and fond of drink. The fight between Telèsphore and André, one of the few physical battles documented in Chopin's works, is described in naturalistic language: "The brute instinct that drives men at each other's throat was awake and stirring in these two. Each saw in the other a thing to be wiped out of his way—out of existence if need be. Passion and blind rage directed the blows which they dealt, and steeled the tension of muscles and clutch of fingers" (497).

Other instincts are also at work. While Zaïda would not have intervened to prevent the drunk André from prevailing over Telèsphore, she knows she has made a mistake in promising to marry him and is happy to return to her family. And Telèsphore is pleased that he can now pursue Zaïda.[45] In its narrative about a young woman turning away from the man she is engaged to so she can seek a fuller life with another, this first story in *A Night in Acadie* is linked to "A No-Account Creole," the first story in *Bayou Folk*. It is linked also with the first and title story of *A Vocation and a Voice*, Chopin's planned third volume of stories. Both narratives were apparently influenced by an opera.

Emily Toth has suggested that Chopin's source for the name Zaïda in "A Night in Acadie" is Margaret Oliphant's novel, *Zaidee*, which Kate Chopin read as a girl (Toth, 52). But more likely Chopin associated the name with one of two operas—the eighteenth-century *Zaïde, reine de Grenade (Zaïde, Queen of Granada)* by Joseph-Nicolas-Pancrace Royer, or *Zaide*, a later work by Wolfgang Amadeus Mozart. The title character in both operas is an independent woman who, claimed by a tyrannical man, prefers another, provoking a violent reaction in the tyrant.

Chopin incorporated references to an opera of Ferdinand Hérold in her novel *The Awakening*. She made another Hérold opera central to her short story "A Vocation and a Voice" and drew on a melodrama later made into an opera for her story "Fedora," both scheduled for inclusion in her projected volume *A Vocation and a Voice*.

In *A Night in Acadie* she begins her turn to opera for inspiration, setting out in a direction that will become stronger in her later volume, one that will take her away from her sources in the people and culture of Louisiana.

A Vocation and a Voice

The balance and harmony of *A Night in Acadie* are gone in *A Vocation and a Voice*, supplanted by the sense of gloom that haunts *The Awakening*, a feeling that fulfillment is beyond reach, that people might find something of what they need to be happy but not everything, that whatever they choose, something just as important must be left behind.

Only one story in the collection is a children's story, and only three or four are set in Louisiana. "Lilacs" takes place in France; "A Vocation and a Voice" drifts from one locale to another (with a few scenes in Louisiana); "The Story of an Hour," "Two Portraits," "The Kiss," and other stories in the volume exist in a virtual location—someplace vague, unnamed, shadowy, not quite real. Several major characters are not given names. Many stories in *A Vocation and a Voice* leave behind a bitter taste, like some of Herman Melville's late works, or Mark Twain's.

Kate Chopin wrote all but one or two of the best *Vocation and a Voice* stories during the same years she wrote the best *Night in Acadie* stories, but she did not include the *Vocation and a Voice* stories in the earlier volume. They would not have fit. She took inspiration for them not from the character of Louisiana Creole or Cajun cultures but from French opera, theater, or literature, from religious organizations, or from generalized American life. Seeking something she could not find in the worlds of her earlier collections, she looked to other cultures for direction.[46]

"A Vocation and a Voice"

Many readers of *The Awakening* have been struck by Chopin's haunting, rhythmic "voice of the sea" passages, and they may remember that a critical step in Edna Pontellier's growth occurs one midnight at Grand Isle when "strange, new voices awoke in her" (946). Edna is "flushed and felt intoxicated with the sound of her own voice" (899), Robert's voice "haunted her memory" (922), and among the last things she hears before she drowns is "her father's voice and her sister Margaret's" (1000). Chopin uses the words *voice* and *voices* over and over in *The Awakening*—at least 43 times.

The power of a voice can be felt throughout Kate Chopin's work. Euphrasie Manton of "A No-Account Creole" cannot decide "whether it was his manner or the tone of his voice or the earnest glance of his dark and deep-set blue eyes" that attracts her to Wallace Offdean (91). Bobinôt in "At the 'Cadian Ball" is enchanted by Calixta's voice "like a rich contralto song, with cadences in it that must have been taught by Satan" (219). Tante Cat'rinette is besieged by the sound of Miss Kitty's voice calling her for help. Mrs. Baroda in "A Respectable Woman" finds herself one night alongside the journalist Gouvernail "drinking in the tones of his voice" (335). Cazeau, the frustrated husband in "Athénaïse," "could not comprehend" why Athénaïse had "attracted him with eyes, with voice, with a hundred womanly ways" (438).

Often in Chopin's works it is not what people say but the voice with which they say it that matters. In many stories, much of what people respond to in other people is carried by cultural habits, socialized behavior, at times by the pitch, tone, rhythm of spoken—or sung—language. Nowhere is that clearer than in the title story of Chopin's third volume of short stories.

"A Vocation and a Voice" (1896) begins with speech, ends with a song, and is driven throughout by the voice of a young woman named Suzima,[47] an itinerant fortune-teller drifting from town to town in the company of Gutro, a disreputable-looking peddler of herbs that he claims can cure all ailments and diseases. The tall, unnamed adolescent boy who must choose between a religious vocation and a life with this young woman meets Suzima by chance at the start of the story, travels with her and Gutro for a season, leaves the two to enter a monastery, then leaps off the wall of the monastery at the close of the story to follow the woman, now traveling alone.

As the title of the story suggests, the boy is drawn to aspects of both a religious vocation and everything implied by the voice of Suzima. Like Wallace Offdean, the boy knows from the start what he wants. He yearns to escape from the overcrowded Donnelly household where he is "an alien member," where "the sordid and puerile impulses of an existence that is not living" make him feel like an "unessential" person. Chopin identifies him with the fall leaves, blown about like "birds with disabled wings making the best of it in a mad frolic." He wants to be out in the "open air," where he purrs with contentment and lapses into "a blessed state of tranquility and contemplation which seemed native to him." He wants to breathe freely, to wander the fields, hills, and woods (521–22).

Part 1

At first he seems able to have his wish. He leaves one day with the movers on an impulse—they need a helper, he has no ties—and he finds his dream immediately: "The days were a gorgeous, golden processional, good and warm with sunshine, and languorous. There were ten, twelve, twenty such days when the earth, sky, wind and water, light and color and sun, and men's souls and their senses and the odor and breath of animals mingled and melted into the harmony of a joyful existence" (526).

But his satisfaction is not sustainable because he thinks of his own soul as different from that of other people's: He "was not innocent or ignorant. He knew the ways of men and viewed them with tranquil indifference, as something external to which no impulse within him responded. His soul had passed through dark places untouched" (530). He sees that Gutro beats Suzima and accepts the violence as inevitable. Yet when the "dark places" start to touch him, when he realizes he cannot keep himself separate, he escapes to a monastery where he builds a wall to keep out ugly aspects of "the ways of men" that he finds in himself.

It is sex that awakens him and his own capacity for violence that he is afraid of. He is an adolescent, a boy, at the start of the story, in spite of his height, and Suzima treats him as one, though she sees him differently after she learns he can serve mass with confidence and recite the prayers in Latin. When he stumbles upon her one day as she is bathing, the image of her naked body burns itself into his consciousness. He and Suzima make love—he is drawn to her by the sight of her bare feet dangling from the wagon they travel in. Now he can no longer ignore Gutro's brutality, and only Suzima's quick reflexes keep him from killing the peddler.

The boy-become-man himself cannot see his way to accepting both his attraction to Suzima—and its resulting violent jealousy of Gutro—and what he thinks of as his spiritual existence. Before his discovery of sex, being under the open sky, especially at night, was in itself enough:

> He was not afraid of the night or of strange places and people. To step his foot out in the darkness, he did not know where, was like tempting the Unknown. Walking thus he felt as if he were alone and holding communion with something mysterious, greater than himself, that reached out from the far distance to touch him—something he called God. Whenever he had gone alone into the parish church at dusk and knelt before the red light of the tabernacle, he had known a feeling akin to this. (530)

56

Before his discovery of sex, he is at peace serving mass and happy in the company of a priest, yet the pull of the countryside and Suzima is stronger. The boy seeks both the religious and the secular life, but he must abandon one part of what is good for him to pursue another.

Chopin drew on nineteenth-century French opera for this story and on French opera and drama for at least two others in *A Vocation and a Voice*. Attendance at the opera is a constant in the world of Chopin's short fiction. People in her first story, "A No-Account Creole," and those in "Charlie," written near the end of her career, attend the opera or perform opera music in their homes. Opera is mentioned in "At Chênière Caminada," "In and Out of Old Natchitoches," "Cavanelle," and other stories.

Recent biographers have not dwelled much on Chopin's interest in opera and theater, but Kitty Garesché, Kate Chopin's childhood friend, wrote that Chopin had a "remarkable" musical memory, that she "would go to the opera of an evening; then the next morning be able to reproduce by ear the parts she liked best." And her early biographer says Chopin "loved the theater and cherished her memories of the magnetic power of the stage."[48]

It is comic opera that Chopin turns to for her fiction, especially the operas of French composer Ferdinand Hérold (1791–1833), which she may have seen or heard during her youth, her marriage trip to Europe, her years in Louisiana, or her life as a writer in St. Louis.[49] *The Awakening* opens with the chattering of a parrot, the singing of birds, and the distant sound of a piano duet from Hérold's famous opera *Zampa* (1831) being played by two young girls, the Farival twins.[50]

"A Vocation and a Voice" echoes with the sound of a "stately refrain" sung by Suzima, who had once done other things besides tell fortunes. She had sung "in the chorus of an opera," she says. The boy is impressed with her singing, thinking "he had never heard anything more beautiful than the full, free notes that came from her throat, filling the vast, woody temple with melody" (525–27).

Chopin must have had Hérold's last opera, *Ludovic* (1833)[51]—or an air from it—in mind as she wrote the story. When the unnamed boy escapes from Suzima, Gutro, and himself by entering a monastery near the end of the narrative, he calls himself Brother "Ludovic." The title character of the opera (set in a village near Rome) is torn between his urgent need to escape from the Pope's pursuing army and his passion for a young woman claimed by another man. Unable to control himself,

Ludovic had wounded the woman because she insists on marrying her cousin.[52]

The opera includes a rondo, "Je vends des scapulaires" ("I sell scapulars"), sung by a woman hawking religious goods—scapulars (cloth sacramental necklaces), rosaries, relics, and certain-to-work prayers (though not fortunes). The woman is joined in her rondo by a chorus. Frédéric Chopin found the air attractive and wrote a piano variation on it.

"Lilacs" and "Two Portraits"

"Lilacs" (1894) is a token of Kate Chopin's fascination with Sarah Bernhardt. It is not known if Chopin saw Bernhardt in person when the great French actress played in American cities during celebrated national tours in the 1880s and 1890s, but Bernhardt's travels were heavily promoted. Newspapers and magazines were filled with stories about the brilliant and scandalous actress—her dazzling stage presence, her magnificent death scenes, her roles as male characters, her string of lovers, her whims, her "chaste sensuality," as one modern critic phrases it.[53] Chopin could not have ignored the media attention.

Adrienne Farival in "Lilacs" (1894), like Sara Bernhardt, is an actress in Paris. Like Bernhardt, she is a sophisticate with money, lovers, fame, fantastic clothing, countless options. Like Bernhardt, she had attended a French convent school and had been a troublemaker there.

But Adrienne Farival, like the title character in *Adrienne Lecouvreur,* a role Bernhardt played in her first American tour, wants something quiet and pure, is tired of her life of society and fashion. She must get away from Paris. Some other actress, perhaps "La Petite Gilberta" (361), will have to play her roles for a few weeks (one of Bernhardt's most famous parts was that of the social butterfly Gilberte in *Froufrou,* a part she performed many times on the American stage).

Though "Lilacs" takes place an ocean away from Louisiana, Kate Chopin's social landscape in the story is familiar. Adrienne is a cosmopolitan Euphrasie Manton of *Bayou Folk* or Athénaïse Miché of *A Night in Acadie,* a woman with a yearning for something more than her life can offer her. Like Euphrasie or Athénaïse—or the boy in "A Vocation and a Voice"—Adrienne is drawn to aspects of the life she knew as a child, but she wants also fulfillment in ways forbidden by the church and respectable society. The narrative details her failure to accommodate the two.

Years earlier, as a pupil at a convent in the French countryside, Adrienne had caused a commotion among the nuns when she climbed the tallest tree on the grounds to seek a glimpse of Paris. Now the smell of lilac blossoms each spring brings her "a perfect fever of agitation" (358), and she rushes back to the convent for two weeks among the nuns.

The convent represents peace for Adrienne, freedom from her hectic life "in the world," as the nuns say. Adrienne lapses into a "heaviness of heart," a "despondency" at times (357–58), and her lovers come and go, but the convent of her youth stays the same, like the lilacs themselves—or at least almost the same. Adrienne is quick to notice even the tiniest alterations from year to year—the stiff wooden chairs seem more polished, a new picture of the Sacré-Coeur hangs over the hall table, the cabbages have been moved from a square on the right of the garden to an oblong bed on the left. Adrienne yearns for permanence and order. At the convent she folds her simple clothes "with great care, placing them on the back of a chair as she had been taught to do when a child." But she needs also the "picturesque disorder" of her room in Paris where her "puzzling and astonishing-looking garments" are "thrown carelessly" around (360–61).

It is the pull of an individual nun as much as the appeal of the communal life that impels Adrienne to seek out the convent each spring. From the first two sentences to the last two, "Lilacs" dwells on the importance of Sister Agathe, the nun "more daring and impulsive than all" who has loved Adrienne since their youth. When word of Adrienne's scandalous life in the city reaches the convent and the "uncompromising, unbending" mother superior (355–56) banishes her forever, it is Sister Agathe whose "face was pressed deep in the pillow in her efforts to smother the sobs that convulsed her frame" (365). For Agathe, Adrienne's absence is "like the spring coming without the sunshine or the song of birds" (358).

As Agathe tells her, "to live one's life along the lines which our dear Lord traces for each one of us, must bring with it resignation and even a certain comfort. You have your household duties, Adrienne, and your music, to which, you say, you continue to devote yourself. And then, there are always good works—the poor—who are always with us—to be relieved; the afflicted to be comforted." It is what Adrienne must expect from this loving friend of her youth whose world is bounded by the convent road, which is "as far as she might go" (359–60). But Adrienne changes the subject. Like Sarah Bernhardt, she has always needed something more. Less famous than Bernhardt, she has managed to attain a sense of balance for a few years, at least, before she is forced to choose.

Kate Chopin does not often include literary references in her fiction. She quotes Whitman in "A Respectable Woman" and Swinburne in *The Awakening,* and in a few other places she mentions a book or an author. The influence of Émile Zola appears in "Lilacs," one more indication of the way Chopin's attention was drifting away from Louisiana. Adrienne Farival threatens to throw one of Zola's books at her maid. "Now I warn you, Sophie," Adrienne says, "the weightiness, the heaviness of Mons. Zola are such that they cannot fail to prostrate you; thankful you may be if they leave you with energy to regain your feet" (362).

Chopin wrote "Lilacs" in 1894, the same year Zola published his novel *Lourdes,* about a young priest who, in an attempt to restore his lost faith, travels with a trainload of sick people to one of the most famous of modern pilgrimage sites, the city in southern France where, many people believe, the Virgin Mary appeared in 1858 to a young peasant girl, Bernadette Soubirous. Kate Chopin read the book—in serialized or book form—and published a review of it the same year.

Chopin seems puzzled in her review about why the Catholic Church would condemn *Lourdes,* but Zola had written the book in part because he feared the Christian revival underway in France during the 1890s and was determined to do what he could to understand the religious impulse and publish his understanding.

As English novelist Angus Wilson argues, Zola often "attacked the emptiness and sentimental emotionalism of the Catholic girls' school, to which even non-practising bourgeois sent their daughters. A rapid, romantic education and an arranged marriage led, he suspected, straight to the adultery of the bored young wife."[54]

One of Zola's most common motifs throughout his works is the way that French families teach their daughters to think of a marriage as a financial association, dooming both partners to loveless relationships and adultery. It is not clear that Adrienne Farival has been married (Sarah Bernhardt was for a brief time), though the nuns believe she has been. Zola's interest in convent schooling would not have been lost on Chopin. She too had studied with Catholic nuns.

A year after she wrote "Lilacs," Chopin divided a woman with Adrienne's needs into two people with the same name and, in a laboratory exercise of naturalistic fiction, probed how childhood environment determines a person's options in later life. "Two Portraits" (1895) has dual sections, each beginning with exactly the same words: "Alberta having looked not very long into life, had not looked very far. She put out her hands to touch things that pleased her and her lips to kiss them. Her eyes were deep brown wells that were drinking, drinking impressions and treasuring them in her soul. They were mysterious eyes and love looked out of them" (462).

Alberta of the first part, titled "The Wanton," grows up with a woman who alternately loves her and beats her. People around her seem "to be always coming and going," always admiring her beauty, fondling her, giving her presents. At 17 she takes her first lover and then settles on a life with men who bring her "love to squander and gold to squander" (462–63).

Alberta of the second part, titled "The Nun," is raised by a "holy woman" who teaches her to subdue the flesh and to concentrate her attention on "the all-wise and all-seeing God." She enters a convent and becomes the most saintly woman there, refreshed by visions, curing people "by the touch of her beautiful hands" (464–66).

"The Falling in Love of Fedora" and "The Kiss"

Sarah Bernhardt toured the United States in 1892 in a melodrama called *Fédora*—the first of seven plays written for her by French dramatist Victorien Sardou—about a Russian princess intent on revenging the murder of her husband.[55] The play was a resounding success, in good part because the role of Fédora fit Bernhardt's public persona perfectly, letting her display what the author asked for—"femininity personified" with "a combination of masculine mind and childish superstitions" (Taranow, 203).

Kate Chopin's title character in "The Falling in Love of Fedora" (1895)[56] is, in her own way, as much an offstage actress as Bernhardt, always in character. She controls her public persona as she does her horse, using the role she plays to hide what she is experiencing. She had "too early in life formed an ideal and treasured it. By this ideal she had measured such male beings as had hitherto challenged her attention, and needless to say she had found them wanting." At age 30 she presents herself as too old for the courting rituals that occupy her brothers and sisters and their guests, though "no one would ever have thought of

it but for her own persistent affectation and idiotic assumption of superior years and wisdom" (467).

She maintains her pose when she meets young Malthers. No one at
the house can guess the extent of her infatuation with him, her "sudden
realization" that the boy she knew eight summers ago has grown up and
is now "a man—in voice, in attitude, in bearing, in every sense—a man"
(467–68). Fedora forgets her "ideal": "She looked at him when he was
near by, she listened for his voice, and took notice and account of what
he said. She sought him out; she selected him when occasion permitted.
She wanted him by her, though his nearness troubled her. There was
uneasiness, restlessness, expectation when he was not there within
sight or sound. There was redoubled uneasiness when he was by—there
was inward revolt, astonishment, rapture, self-contumely; a swift, fierce
encounter betwixt thought and feeling" (468).

No one can guess the reason for her insistence on driving the cart and
meeting the train that is bringing his sister for a social visit—not the
people at the house, not the workmen at the station, not the girl herself.
Fedora's bearing—"elegant, composed, reserved—betrayed nothing
emotional as she tramped the narrow platform, whip in hand, and occasionally offered a condescending word to the mail man or the sleepy
agent" (468).

She plays her part like a professional. When Miss Malthers arrives,
she finds "vivid, poignant" the "suggestive resemblance" of the girl to
her brother. But she recites her lines as always. "You know, dear child,"
she says in her older, wiser voice, "I want you to feel completely at home
with us," and she encircles the girl's shoulders with her left hand as she
holds the reins of the horse with her right (469).

Even for Sarah Bernhardt, Fedora's actions in the closing sentences of
the story would have been scandalous: "When the girl looked up into
her face, with murmured thanks, Fedora bent down and pressed a long,
penetrating kiss upon her mouth. Malthers's sister appeared astonished,
and not too well pleased. Fedora, with seemingly unruffled composure,
gathered the reins, and for the rest of the way stared steadily ahead of
her between the horses' ears" (469).

Fedora's kiss may be meant for Malthers—people give and receive
such ambiguous kisses in "A No-Account Creole," "A Respectable
Woman," and "Athénaïse"—an example, as Joyce Dyer says, of repressive displacement.[57] But it also may be meant for his sister, as Nancy E.
Rogers notes (Rogers, 36), or as Susan Koppelman argues in her anthology of nineteenth-century lesbian stories.[58] The role Fedora plays lets

her conceal her intentions from her family and friends, from Malther's sister, and, perhaps, from herself as well.

There is nothing ambiguous about the kiss in an earlier story, though the recipient in "The Kiss" (1894) manages to convince the young millionaire she would like to marry that it was only a mark of friendship.

Nathalie, too, acts a part, though she has not always done so. Before she set her sights on the "rather insignificant and unattractive" but "enormously rich" Brantain, she apparently had a passionate relationship with a man named Harvey. When Harvey enters a dark room and sees Nathalie—but not Brantain—he rushes over to her. "Before she could suspect his intention, for she did not realize that he had not seen her visitor—he pressed an ardent, lingering kiss upon her lips" (379).

Nathalie is a convincing enough actress to later persuade Brantain that she and Harvey have "always been like cousins—like brother and sister," and at her wedding she feels "like a chess player who, by the clever handling of his pieces, sees the game taking the course intended" when her husband sends Harvey over to kiss her. But Harvey refuses the kiss, telling her he has given up kissing women. "It's dangerous," he says.

"Well," the story concludes, "she had Brantain and his million left. A person can't have everything in this world; and it was a little unreasonable of her to expect it" (380–81).

"Her Letters"

"Her Letters" is a companion piece to "The Story of an Hour" (discussed in the introduction to this volume), both written in 1894 and both published in *Vogue*. Again a married woman with a life-threatening physical condition locks herself in a room, loses herself in reveries of a different life, then dies suddenly. Mrs. Mallard in the earlier story looks out a window at her future without the husband who, she believes, has just been killed in a train crash. The unnamed woman in "Her Letters" looks into a writing desk at her past with the lover whose letters, she believes, she must now burn to prevent her husband from finding them after her death. Mrs. Mallard dies a few minutes later when her husband appears in the doorway. The woman in "Her Letters" dies a few months later as she tries to reach the letters she refused to destroy because they are all that has sustained her during her declining years.

It is springtime and the sky is blue in "The Story of an Hour." Mrs. Mallard's life has hardly begun; the first signs of growth are just appearing. It is autumn and the sky "leaden" in "Her Letters" (398), but though the woman's present is bleak, her life has passed through rich seasons of fulfillment. There had been "the days when she felt she had lived" (400). Her lover "had changed the water in her veins to wine, whose taste had brought delirium to both of them." Even now his letters move her, especially the "most precious and most imprudent" letter. It has seared her consciousness: "Every word of untempered passion had long ago eaten its way into her brain; and . . . stirred her still to-day, as it had done a hundred times before when she thought of it. She crushed it between her palms when she found it. She kissed it again and again. With her sharp white teeth she tore the far corner from the letter, where the name was written; she bit the torn scrap and tasted it between her lips and upon her tongue like some god-given morsel" (399).

Mrs. Mallard's life in "The Story of an Hour" and the woman's life in "Her Letters" each unfolds in about a thousand words, but "Her Letters" continues for another two thousand words because it shifts its focus to the husband, so the bleakness in the story—the feeling of "no gleam, no rift, no promise" (398)—is even more descriptive of the man's life than the woman's. Mrs. Mallard's husband learns nothing of what is in his wife's consciousness. When her life ends, so does the narrative. But the woman in "Her Letters" has left a note for her husband asking him to destroy her letters unopened, and although he grants her wish, he is so haunted by the thought that "there is but one secret which a woman would choose to have die with her" that he drowns himself (404). A "man-instinct of possession"[59] drives him to seek out his wife's lover and, unable to identify him, to take his own life.

A romantic sense of a "dual life," as Edna Pontellier in *The Awakening* understands it, "the outward existence which conforms, the inner life which questions," pervades *A Vocation and a Voice*, though sometimes, as in "Her Letters" or "Lilacs," two separate existences are "outward." They are hidden from each other and incompatible—but they are lived, not only imagined, as are Mrs. Mallard's reveries or Edna Pontellier's adolescent fantasies about romantic men. The husband in "Her Letters" cannot survive with the idea that his wife had a second existence. His "manhood" is threatened (405) because he sees her lover as his "enemy" (403). Like the "uncompromising, unbending" mother superior in "Lilacs," he expects complete loyalty—everything or nothing.

His hurtling himself into the river to find "peace and sweet repose" from the unbearable knowledge that his wife shared herself with another validates the woman's determination to keep her second life a secret (405). She does not want to inflict "pain" and "anguish" on this man "whose tenderness and years of devotion had made him, in a manner, dear to her." She has been what she could be for him, while responding with eagerness to the man who "had changed the water in her veins to wine" (399). Her husband has known her as "cold and passionless, but true, and watchful of his comfort and his happiness" (401).[60]

Dual lives are not often reconciled in *A Vocation and a Voice,* balance not usually reached, harmony seldom achieved. The atmosphere of many stories in the volume has "no gleam, no rift, no promise." In "Her Letters," one person's fulfillment leads to another's destruction.

"A Morning Walk" and "The Night Came Slowly"

Chopin's last book of short stories is not unrelenting gloom. There are touches of brightness, with one story phrased in language reminiscent of *Bayou Folk.*

Archibald of "A Morning Walk" (1897) is a 40-year-old man who wanders into an Easter service at a church in the little village where he lives. He has been an intrusive observer more than a participant in the life of his village. He studies insects and dissects flowers, but he does not remember the name of a comely 20-year-old village girl when he meets her on Easter morning. He yearns for some system through which various young females might, like flowers and insects, be easily classified so he can tell one from another. On his morning walks, he captures butterflies and grasshoppers, and with his stick he displaces pebbles, stones, weeds, and flowers. Even his village is described as if it were an extension of his actions, an imposition upon nature: the houses rest upon a lofty shelf chiseled into the side of a mountain.

Yet Archibald is not satisfied. He is unable to reconcile what he knows about the small world of insects and flowers with what he finds in the community about him. He studies books about "peoples long since gathered to the earth and the elements" (567). His place in the universe troubles him, and he senses something is happening to him. As he moves along the road, he "now and again . . . straightened his shoulders and shook his head with an impatient movement, as might some proud animal which rebels against an unaccustomed burden" (566). The odors of flowers combine with the sounds and colors of spring to disturb him. He is moved by the pretty village girl whose lilies he offers to carry to the church. When he sits down, not understanding why, alongside her, the words of the minister, "I am the Resurrection and the Life," penetrate his being (569).

Archibald looks out the window, ignoring the service in progress, but the minister's sentence brings into focus for him "the poet's vision, of the life that is within and the life that is without, pulsing in unison, breathing the harmony of an undivided existence" (569). The phrase describes part of what people in Kate Chopin's universe are reaching for. But Chopin is not offering Christianity as a force that might harmonize or unify aspects of life. Archibald's "vision" is that of a poet, not a religious devotee. It is more the result of spring flowers and colors and the beautiful girl next to him than the words of the minister.[61]

"The Night Came Slowly" (1894) is more representative of Kate Chopin's treatment of religion in *A Vocation and a Voice*. The unusual first-person narrative with Whitmanesque language runs less than three hundred words:

> I am losing my interest in human beings; in the significance of their lives and their actions. Some one has said it is better to study one man than ten books. I want neither books nor men; they make me suffer. Can one of them talk to me like the night—the Summer night? Like the stars or the caressing wind?
>
> The night came slowly, softly, as I lay out there under the maple tree. It came creeping, creeping stealthily out of the valley, thinking I did not notice. And the outlines of trees and foliage nearby blended in one black mass and the night came stealing out from them, too, and from the east and west, until the only light was in the sky, filtering through the maple leaves and a star looking down through every cranny.
>
> The night is solemn and it means mystery.
>
> Human shapes flitted by like intangible things. Some stole up like little mice to peep at me. I did not mind. My whole being was abandoned to the soothing and penetrating charm of the night.
>
> The katydids began their slumber song: they are at it yet. How wise they are. They do not chatter like people. They tell me only: "sleep, sleep, sleep." The wind rippled the maple leaves like little warm love thrills.
>
> Why do fools cumber the Earth! It was a man's voice that broke the necromancer's spell. A man came to-day with his "Bible Class." He is

detestable with his red cheeks and bold eyes and coarse manner and speech. What does he know of Christ? Shall I ask a young fool who was born yesterday and will die tomorrow to tell me things of Christ? I would rather ask the stars: they have seen him. (366)

For decades many critics have argued that Kate Chopin fell into a malaise after 1899 because of harsh reviews of *The Awakening*. But Chopin wrote almost all the best stories in *A Vocation and a Voice* between 1894 and 1896, during some of her most productive years, before she began work on her great novel. The sense that happiness cannot be reached, unity and balance cannot be had—the feeling that if something is gained, something else must be lost—pervades the stories.

Children's Stories

The boundary in the *Bayou Folk* story "Madame Célestin's Divorce" has immense power. Lawyer Paxton cannot persuade the pretty Creole woman to cross it. But in an earlier story, "Beyond the Bayou" (1891), in the same volume, Kate Chopin had created a touching work about a boundary even more frightening for the woman whose existence it encloses, though La Folle—everyone calls her the crazy one[62]—overcomes her "morbid and insane dread" of crossing the "imaginary line" she had built as a terrorized child (175–77).

For 30 or so years La Folle had refused to venture past the bayou that encircles her cabin because she had been paralyzed by the childhood memory of "P'tit Maître, black with power and crimson with blood" staggering into her mother's cabin, "his pursuers close at his heels." Though P'tit Maître had grown into middle age, fathered several children, and moved the plantation cabins to the other side of the bayou, La Folle had stayed behind by herself, raising her cotton, corn, and tobacco, and fascinating P'tit Maître's children with her wonderful stories about things that always happen "yonda, beyon' de bayou" (175–76).

When the little 10-year-old she loves the best, the child she calls "Chéri," accidentally shoots himself in the leg near her cabin, she takes him in her arms and rushes to the border, wailing for help that does not come:

> La Folle gave a last despairing look around her. Extreme terror was upon her. She clasped the child close against her breast, where he could feel her heart beat like a muffled hammer. Then shutting her eyes, she ran suddenly down the shallow bank of the bayou, and never stopped till she had climbed the opposite shore.
>
> She stood there quivering an instant as she opened her eyes. Then she plunged into the footpath through the trees.
>
> She spoke no more to Chéri, but muttered constantly, "Bon Dieu, ayez pitié La Folle! Bon Dieu, ayez pitié moi!" (177–78)

Her prayers for help sustain her enough to reach the plantation manor where she deposits Chéri in his father's arms and collapses. But she returns early the next day and sits on the steps of the veranda waiting for Chéri to wake up. "A look of wonder and deep content crept into her face as she watched for the first time the sun rise upon the new, the beautiful world beyond the bayou" (180).[63]

"Beyond the Bayou" has become increasingly popular among anthologists and critics. It appears in three Chopin paperbacks and several college textbooks,[64] and a book of Chopin criticism is called *Kate Chopin Reconsidered: Beyond the Bayou.* But critics and anthologists do not always note that Kate Chopin wrote the story for children, that she published it in *Youth's Companion* before including it in *Bayou Folk.* The story is representative of the blurry line separating Kate Chopin's adult stories from her children's works.

Historians speak of there being a moment in the development of a modern Western culture when, because of society's need for an educated citizenry, childhood emerges as a separate domain, structured differently from that of adulthood, hidden much of the time from the view of many adults.[65] That moment had arrived in the United States by the nineteenth century. With it came the publication of books and magazines written for the enlightenment or entertainment—more than for the moral instruction—of children. Many nineteenth-century Americans wrote for children as well as adults—Washington Irving, Nathaniel Hawthorne, Louisa May Alcott, Sara Orne Jewett, and Mark Twain, among them.

About a third of Kate Chopin's one hundred short stories are children's stories. Fifteen were published in *Youth's Companion* or *Harper's Young People,* popular children's magazines of the day. At least 16 others were accepted by those magazines but not published, refused by them, or built around subject matter similar to that in the published stories.[66]

About half the stories in *Bayou Folk* are children's stories, as are about a third of those in *A Night in Acadie,* though only one story in *A Vocation and a Voice* was intended for children. Seventeen of Chopin's first 30 stories are children's stories, as are 11 of her last 30. Chopin alternated between writing for adults and for children throughout her career.

Just what an author includes in children's stories depends on when and where the stories were written, the state of the publishing field at the time, the attitudes of parents about what is appropriate for children to read, and other factors. But most nineteenth- and twentieth-century readers, in America and Great Britain at least, seem to believe that because children are developing more than developed, because they lack the maturity to filter and contextualize what stories say, an author setting out to write for them has a responsibility to choose subjects with some restraint.[67]

Kate Chopin discusses the matter in an essay published in St. Louis in 1897:

> The question of how much or how little knowledge of life should be withheld from the youthful mind is one which need only be touched upon here. It is a subject about which there exists a diversity of opinion with the conservative element no doubt, greatly in preponderance. As a rule the youthful, untrained nature is left to gather wisdom as it comes along in a thousand-and-one ways and in whatever form it may present itself to the intelligent, the susceptible, the observant. In this respect experience is perhaps an abler instructor than direct enlightenment from man or woman; for it works by suggestion. There are many phases and features of life which cannot, or rather should not be expounded, demonstrated, presented to the youthful imagination as cold facts, for it is safe to assert they are not going to be accepted as such. It is moreover robbing youth of its privilege to gather wisdom as the bee gathers honey. (713)

Chopin complains in her essay about efforts to block children's access to Thomas Hardy's *Jude the Obscure* (1895), which apparently had been withdrawn from St. Louis libraries, and she reaches in her children's stories—as she does in her adult stories—for what she calls "true life and true art," for "human existence in its subtle, complex, true meaning, stripped of the veil with which ethical and conventional standards have draped it" (691–92).

Nevertheless, her stories share a good part of what scholars argue is characteristic of much children's literature in the nineteenth century and today. Perry Nodelman writes that even very complex children's stories like Robert Louis Stevenson's *Treasure Island* (1883) or E. B. White's *Charlotte's Web* (1952) share "a fascination with the same basic sets of opposite ideas, and a propensity for bringing them into balance, so that both can be included in a vision of what life is." "All in some way combine what one wishes for with what one must accept, all deal with freedom and constriction, home and exile, escape and acceptance, and all create balances between these extremes."[68]

Chopin is fascinated with balance in many of her adult stories. Other concerns of her adult fiction appear also in her children's work, and some different themes and motifs come up as well.

At least 12 children's stories emphasize the poverty so often present in her work in general. The boy in "For Marse Chouchoute" (1891), Chopin's first children's story, supports his mother and himself by carrying mail pouches to a train station, while the boys in "Mamouche" (1893) and "Alexandre's Wonderful Experience" (1900) are orphans rescued by wealthy adults. The girl in "A Very Fine Fiddle" (1891) sells her father's priceless violin to buy food and shoes for her siblings, the child in "A Little Country Girl" (1899) wants just enough money to go to a circus, while the young woman in "Polly" (1902), Chopin's last children's story and last published story, uses a hundred-dollar windfall to send groceries, coal, and some conveniences to her mother and sister. A desperate poverty drives the narrative in "Love on the Bon-Dieu" and "A Rude Awakening" (both 1891), and the dignified pride that sometimes masks poor living conditions is visible in "Boulôt and Boulotte" (1891) and "The Wood-Choppers" (1901).

Several stories focus on 16-, 17-, and 18-year-old girls crossing from childhood to adulthood. "The Maid of Saint Phillipe" (1891), "A Rude Awakening" (1891), "Loka" (1892), "Aunt Lympy's Interference" (1896), and "Charlie" (1900) all explore matters of identity, freedom, and responsibility. The longest and most complex is the last, which resembles "Athénaïse" in its narrative of an independent, unmanageable country girl who matures through experiences in New Orleans and returns to the country to take up the responsibilities of an adult—though it is her father, not her husband, she returns to, and it is his need, not hers, that brings her back.

A string of stories is about the surprising but ultimately redeeming behavior of an eccentric individual. "Beyond the Bayou" (1891), "A Matter of Prejudice" (1893), and "Ripe Figs" (1892) are the best known of the group, but "After the Winter" (1891) and "A Turkey Hunt" (1892) have a similar orientation.

Two of the best children's stories are set on holidays and focus on an adult's need for renewed human contact. "After the Winter" describes the Easter Sunday change in a man who had returned from the Civil War 25 years earlier to find that his wife had deserted him. "A Matter of Prejudice" follows the Christmas Day trip by a French woman to the home of a son whom she had banished 10 years before because he had married an American woman. "Madame Martel's Christmas Eve" (1896) also has a holiday setting, as does "Love on the Bon-Dieu" (1891).

Other stories deal with lost memory—"A Wizard from Gettysburg" and "A Rude Awakening" (both 1891)—or a search for identity and security—"The Bênitous' Slave," "A Little Free-Mulatto," and "Loka" (all 1892).

Critics have given little thought to Chopin's—or some other American writers'—children's stories.[69] Peter Hunt, who writes about children's books, has wondered about why such works are so often "invisible in the literary world":

> It is common to find that adults are wary about approaching children's books critically (approaching them emotionally is another matter). This may be because they fear the loss of a valued part of childhood—that the spell will be broken; or, as Ursula Le Guin suggested, because the modern adult has been taught to downgrade the imagination; or because, in the critical hierarchy, children's books are so trivial that to study them is not a legitimate activity. . . .
>
> In short, with the exception of those of us who can hide, as it were, behind 'working with children', we suspect that children's literature is a kind of private vice. . . . Even for the confident, there is a danger that, as Perry Nodelman put it, 'people who take literature seriously [think that] children's literature can only be important if it isn't really for children at all, but actually secret pop-Zen for fuzzyminded grownups'. (Hunt, 2)

Whatever the reasons for their being ignored, Kate Chopin's stories for children are attractive works of fiction. They are gentler, more playful, than some of Chopin's adult works, perhaps because children's fiction has always drawn the world more as adults think it should be than as they know it is. The stories build, like other children's stories, upon themes of maturation and development—"what one wishes for [and] what one must accept . . . freedom and constriction, home and exile." And several are powerful, beautiful works. "Beyond the Bayou," "A Matter of Prejudice," "Ripe Figs," and a few other stories will haunt the imagination of the children—or the adults—who read them.

Uncollected Stories

A Vocation and a Voice is a dark book. Kate Chopin would produce no more *Bayou Folks*. But in 1896 and 1898 she wrote two brilliant stories, two of the finest to emerge from turn-of-the-century America, stories with a *Bayou Folk* brightness, though of a more complex nature.

Vogue published "A Pair of Silk Stockings" (1896). No magazine would have published "The Storm" (1898), as Joyce Carol Oates points out, because of its sexual frankness.[70] Chopin apparently did not even try to send it out to publishers. Not until 1969 did it appear in print. Neither "A Pair of Silk Stockings" nor "The Storm" was meant for an anthology. Neither would have fit in *A Vocation and a Voice*.

Both stories are wondrously alive—passionate, joyful, even ecstatic, bursting with life—but of a different character from the narratives of Chopin's early work. They are understated, quietly confident, mature, masterful, at peace with ambiguity. They glory in the rightness of instinctive dispositions.

Both narratives are played out in just a few hours and are set in motion by the appearance of an outside force—an unexplained financial windfall in the first, a violent thunderstorm in the second.

"A Pair of Silk Stockings"

What Kate Chopin calls "impulse" runs strong in many of her works, but seldom does it dominate a narrative so completely as it does in "A Pair of Silk Stockings."

Little Mrs. Sommers, as the narrator refers to her, lets impulse guide her throughout her afternoon in the city as she sets out to spend a rare 15-dollar windfall on necessities for her "little brood" of children. She has for days carefully calculated her plans to buy shoes and percale and socks and hats for her children, but as she sits famished and exhausted at a counter in front of some silk stockings on sale, she instead gives herself over for the afternoon to dispositions planted during "better days" before her marriage (500): "She was not going through any acute mental process or reasoning with herself, nor was she striving to explain to her satisfaction the motive of her action. She was not thinking at all. She seemed for the time to be taking a rest from that laborious and fatiguing function and to have abandoned herself to some mechanical impulse that directed her actions and freed her of responsibility" (502).

Her reaction to the silk fabric is immediate and physical. The "soft, sheeny luxurious" silk stockings bring "hectic blotches" to her cheeks—so she buys a pair and revels in the "touch of the raw silk to her flesh." She buys "excellent" boots of a "stylish" fit, kid gloves, and some expensive magazines "such as she had been accustomed to read in the days when she had been accustomed to other pleasant things" (501–3).

Following "the impulse that was guiding her," she finds a restaurant with "spotless damask and shining crystal, and soft-stepping waiters serving people of fashion" where she eats a "nice and tasty bite" followed by a crème-frappée, a glass of Rhine wine, and black coffee. And she uses the remainder of her 15 dollars to attend a matinee performance at the theater: "She gathered in the whole—stage and players and people in one wide impression, and absorbed it and enjoyed it. She laughed at the comedy and wept—she and the gaudy woman next to her wept over the tragedy. And they talked a little together over it. And the gaudy woman wiped her eyes and sniffled on a tiny square of filmy, perfumed lace and passed little Mrs. Sommers her box of candy" (503–4).

When the play is over, "it was like a dream ended" for Mrs. Sommers, and even the man "with keen eyes" opposite her in the cable car she takes cannot know what she is thinking, cannot "detect a poignant wish, a powerful longing that the cable car would never stop anywhere, but go on and on with her forever" (504).

As Barbara Ewell notes: "That Mrs. Sommers is filled with regret is clear. But regret for what? for the self-indulgence of a day with the money of a windfall? for the dissipation of an illusion of well-being? for the impossibility of freedom? for the life she has chosen? for the hungry, clamoring children who await her? Chopin lets us guess. The changes in Mrs. Sommers possess an impenetrable interiority" (Ewell, 120).

That interiority may be impenetrable for Mrs. Sommers, too. The 15 dollars she had come upon (described in the first sentence of the story) is for her a "very large amount of money" (500). We know nothing about what happened to her husband or to the wealth of her "better days." Mrs. Sommers does not think about it. She concentrates on the present, following the instincts she does not consciously control.

"The Storm"

"The Storm" takes place five years after the cyclone that ruined Alcée Laballière's rice crop in "At the 'Cadian Ball." Alcée refers to the storm in this story as a cyclone, too, and his comment is one of the ways in which the narratives resemble each other, the second a continuation of the first.[71]

Yet in one fundamental sense, the stories could not be more different. The storm in "At the 'Cadian Ball" sets off a chain of events that clarifies the social atmosphere, resulting in two marriages solidifying the social position of Alcée and Clarisse, the Creole couple, and that of Bobinôt and Calixta, the 'Cadian couple. The scandal threatened by a liaison between Alcée (the Creole) and Calixta (the 'Cadian with some Cuban blood) is averted.[72] Clarisse lays claim to her kinsman Alcée, and Calixta accepts the long-standing marriage offer from Bobinôt. Balance and harmony are achieved, social stability reigns.

The thunderstorm in the later story also clears the air and brings about a new harmony but leaves the social landscape ambiguous, confused, unstable. The events of the story are set in motion by chance and impulse. Calixta is at home alone in "The Storm" as the summer thunderstorm draws near. Bobinôt and their four-year-old son have decided to wait out the rain at a store in the neighboring village. Alcée, also alone because his wife and children are spending their first vacation away from the plantation, and also seeking shelter from the storm, finds himself near the cabin of Calixta. The torrential rain and the wind force him to join her inside the cabin.

The two stand quietly for a few moments watching the downpour through a window, but a close bolt of lightning startles the already nervous Calixta, and she falls backward into Alcée's arms. For both, the unexpected physical contact revives memories of their earlier passion for each other. While the storm rages outside they go into the cabin's bedroom and make love with a joyful abandonment.

As the rain ends, Alcée rides off and Calixta laughs aloud as she bids him good-bye. The final few paragraphs of the story describe first the return of Calixta's husband to his cheerful wife and then Alcée's letter to Clarisse, telling her she should feel free to stay longer if she is enjoying her vacation. "So the storm passed," the famous last sentence of the story reads, "and every one was happy" (596).

"At the 'Cadian Ball" emphasizes the social forces at work on Alcée. When the Creole planter seeks a kindred spirit after his encounter with the coldness of Clarisse and the heat of the cyclone, he finds himself hemmed in by other people. He is interrupted three times during the several minutes he manages to spend alone with Calixta, and the narrative emphasizes the 'Cadians' disapproval of Calixta's ways with men. Alcée and Calixta are prevented by their community from exploring their passion for each other.

"The Storm" emphasizes the power of nature. Social forces are suspended. Alcée first and then Calixta with him accept the storm in the same spirit that they accept their attraction to each other. The wildness of the elements makes Calixta laugh as she clings to Alcée. The two behave with the childlike naturalness of Maman-Nainaine in "Ripe Figs." They are fulfilled through their contact with each other.

"Every one was happy," the last sentence says—Alcée and Calixta because after five years of marriage to other people they have joyously submitted to the sexual passions they had fled from before; Clarisse because Alcée has encouraged her to stay longer on vacation, which she is pleased to do; and Bobinôt because Calixta welcomes him home after the storm in the best of humor, without her usual "over-scrupulous" concern about the mud on his clothes (595–96).

But the harmony in "The Storm," the sense of personal happiness and social balance is—like the feeling at the close of "A Pair of Silk Stockings"—tentative, temporary, limited. It emerges from Alcée's and Calixta's willingness to follow impulses that they had resisted five years earlier.[73]

"The Storm" became popular as soon as it appeared in Per Seyersted's *Complete Works of Kate Chopin* in 1969, in good part because of what Seyersted calls its "Whitmanesque pervasive erotic atmosphere" (Seyersted, 167). Chopin's language is startling in its simplicity, directness, and beauty.

When Calixta falls back into Alcée's arms, the planter "pushed her hair back from her face that was warm and steaming": "Her lips were as red and moist as pomegranate seed. Her white neck and a glimpse of her full, firm bosom disturbed him powerfully. As she glanced up at him the fear in her liquid blue eyes had given place to a drowsy gleam that unconsciously betrayed a sensuous desire. He looked down into her eyes and there was nothing for him to do but to gather her lips in a kiss" (594).

For 25 years, critics have marveled at Kate Chopin's freedom in continuing the scene. The remarkable description of Calixta and Alcée making love emerges from Chopin's personal experience and her love of

Walt Whitman—and from her intimate familiarity with the language of Maupassant and Zola, the music of Chopin and Hérold, and the fabric of daily life in France and the Creole regions of Louisiana. Calixta's lips, Chopin writes, "seemed in a manner free to be tasted, as well as her round, white throat and her whiter breasts":

> They did not heed the crashing torrents, and the roar of the elements made her laugh as she lay in his arms. She was a revelation in that dim, mysterious chamber; as white as the couch she lay upon. Her firm, elastic flesh that was knowing for the first time its birthright, was like a creamy lily that the sun invites to contribute its breath and perfume to the undying life of the world.
>
> The generous abundance of her passion, without guile or trickery, was like a white flame which penetrated and found response in depths of his own sensuous nature that had never yet been reached.
>
> When he touched her breasts they gave themselves up in quivering ecstasy, inviting his lips. Her mouth was a fountain of delight. And when he possessed her, they seemed to swoon together at the very borderland of life's mystery. (594–95)

"At the 'Cadian Ball" is a strong nineteenth-century story. "The Storm" is America's first great twentieth-century short story. It turns its back on the usual literary treatment of women. Calixta is—as critics have argued—a modern woman breaking free of assigned female roles. And the natural forces in the work "refresh" everybody, as Bert Bender points out: "Kate Chopin's principle here, as usual, is that freedom nourishes" (Bender, 265).

The two lovers in "The Storm" are brilliantly imagined, vibrantly alive human beings. They reach impulsively out of the depths of their existence, out of their early lives, out of all the experiences that made them the people they are, for what they want, what they need, what for them is life itself, their "birthright"—not selfishly, not unaware of the risks and costs, not with the intention of hurting anybody, but with a lust for life itself, with an ecstatic acceptance of what the moment is offering them, with trust and peace and hope.

"Charlie"

Kate Chopin wrote only a few short stories after composing "The Storm" and after the publication of *The Awakening*. "Charlie" (1900) is the strongest. It is Chopin's last important story and her longest story.[74]

It draws motifs from *Bayou Folk* narratives about young people seeking occupations and companions. It resembles "Athénaïse" from *A Night in Acadie* in its narrative movement from a plantation to the city of New Orleans and back and its focus on a headstrong young girl. While it abandons the impetus in *A Vocation and a Voice* to turn away from Louisiana for inspiration, it shares with "A Pair of Silk Stockings" and "The Storm" a feeling that a person can in the end have what she wants and needs, though the price for having it in "Charlie" is high.

The story is about a 17-year-old girl's love for her father and her determination to do what is good for him. Although the title character is a girl—not a boy, despite her masculine nickname, her short hair, and her love of target shooting and horseback riding at breakneck speed—the narrative is focused from the first sentence to the last on the importance to the girl of the affection and approval of her father. Charlie "really felt," the story reads, "that nothing made much difference so long as her father was happy" (643).

Charlie (her given name is Charlotte) had taught herself to ride and shoot and fish after her mother died, to be "untiring and fearless," thereby filling the place of "that ideal son" her father "had always hoped for and that had never come" (644). She refuses to follow her other sisters in learning to dance and play the piano, she resists the oppressive order of the tutor her father has hired for his daughters, and she marshals her sisters to persuade her father that he should not remarry. When her undisciplined behavior becomes painful for her father, she repents, but "her actions were reprehensible in her own eyes only so far as they interfered with his peace of mind" (643).

The outsider whose appearance sets the narrative in motion is a young New Orleans man on a business mission. Charlie accidentally wounds him while target shooting, so her father, despite his belief in the "ultimate integrity of his daughter's intentions" (650), feels compelled to send Charlie to a highly disciplined young ladies' seminary in the city.

But while Charlie consciously sets out to please her father in a new role, to learn to dance and to make her hands as white and soft as her older sister's, she is guided now by "the feminine instinct" (656), though she so covers herself with laces and jewels that her sister and aunt marvel over her "vulgar instincts" (657).

Charlie does nothing halfway. She falls in love with the young man she has wounded, and when her older sister announces her engagement to him, she fires off a volley of denunciation out of a "savage impulse"

(667) that leaves her shaken with remorse, but she then gives her sister her most precious possession, her mother's diamond engagement ring. And when her father loses an arm in a near-fatal accident at his sugar mill, his "beloved daughter" (653) leaves school, refuses the possibility to go abroad with her aunt, and tells the neighbor who loves her that although she likes him "better than any one," she must postpone marriage until her little sisters are grown because she "couldn't dream of leaving Dad without a right arm" (669). Her experiences have "left her a woman" (667). She becomes the mistress of the plantation. The story is touching and tender, but it has a melancholy core.

Per Seyersted says a Freudian would find a "fixation" in Charlie's relationship with her father (Seyersted, 183), but Anne M. Blythe rightly objects to the implications, arguing that "there is no hint of anything abnormal or unhealthy in the feelings of either, no suggestion that this healthy father-daughter relationship is in any way delaying or hampering her maturing as a young woman or growing in need and ability to respond to other men."[75]

By giving her mother's diamond ring to her older sister (it is not clear why that ring is hers in the first place), Charlie repudiates her desire to reproduce her parents' life with the New Orleans businessman. In electing to manage the plantation and postpone marriage, she is free to be the daughter, the son, the companion, the best friend her father needs.[76]

Chopin's Audience, Chopin's Legacy

Kate Chopin came late to writing, and her career was short. Besides her stories, she wrote two novels—*At Fault* and *The Awakening*[77]—poetry, literary essays (excerpts are included in Part 2 of this volume), and journals. About a third of her stories have been discussed here in some detail and another third, the children's stories, touched upon briefly. Much of the remaining third is made up of apprentice works or stories that Daniel Aaron calls the work of the "public" Chopin (Aaron, 348), the Chopin who was eager to please, eager to build a career for herself. Perhaps some of those stories will speak more persuasively to readers in future generations.[78]

Chopin was not widely known by scholars or the American public until she was swept up by the force of the feminist movement in the 1970s, but she was not entirely ignored before then. Anthologists included 8 of her short stories in 11 volumes published from the 1920s to the 1960s and some of those volumes were reissued many times (Koloski, 19–26). Several of America's finest critics from the 1920s to the 1960s praised her work—Fred Lewis Pattee in 1922, Arthur Hobson Quinn in 1936, Van Wyck Brooks in 1952, and Kenneth Eble in 1956. Major critics were writing about *The Awakening* throughout the 1960s— Edmund Wilson in 1962, Warner Berthoff in 1965, Larzer Ziff and Stanley Kauffmann in 1966, George Arms in 1967, and Lewis Leary in 1968.[79] Per Seyersted's famous biography in 1969 was the fulfillment of, not the beginning of, the Chopin revival.

To be sure, these early scholars and anthologists, most of them male, were products of their cultures. It is easy to look through what they have written, find an offensive remark, and dismiss their work out of hand. But each was moved by Kate Chopin's power, each touched by the beauty of her work, each led to insights that have something to offer us today. The eminent feminist critic Elaine Showalter notes that "we owe the rediscovery of Chopin's work not to American women writers but to male literary critics from France and Norway as well as from the United States."[80]

Unfortunately, Kate Chopin was not well served by Daniel Rankin, her first biographer, a Catholic priest who published his study of her work in 1932. Rankin was, as Daniel Aaron phrased it in 1971, "disqualified by taste and temperament from doing justice to the original qualities of Kate Chopin's mind" (Aaron, 342). He liked many of her short stories but was disturbed by *The Awakening* and, since no other biography appeared until Seyersted's in 1969, an entire generation of scholars accepted much of what he said, and one of America's great novels went unread until recent decades.

Chopin's legacy rests solidly upon the reputation of that novel. Yet, as this volume suggests, many of her short stories reach out to readers at the turn of the twenty-first century. They are clear and accessible. They are warm, compact, subtle, charming. They can surprise, entertain, illuminate, challenge, move to tears.

Chopin shared with other nineteenth-century American writers the impulse to stay close to home in creating her imaginative universe but to look abroad for ways of understanding the truth of what she had made. She wrote about the region and the people she knew but drew inspiration from France. Often an outsider herself, she populated her stories with outsiders, people who carry different cultural values, who upset the social status quo and impel others to seek a new way of life.

If Chopin sought to change anything about the world, it was its representation, the way it is seen. She was aware of economic, psychological, biological, and other forces but did not routinely treat them as stresses and drives over which people have little or no control, as did many of her contemporaries in Europe and America. In her fiction, people shape actions freely from within themselves, though those selves have been shaped by the people among whom they have lived. For Chopin, a person is "in the social world" but the social world is in the person, as some sociologists today would say.[81]

Kate Chopin understands "human existence," one of her favorite phrases, as driven by a yearning for something she often calls "rights of existence"—a chance for harmony and balance, rich social and cultural possibilities, and physical and material freedom and fulfillment. Although she is a complex writer and some of her work is ambiguous, she has a remarkably clear view of people's positions in their cultures, of *her* position in her two cultures. She is among the least naïve of American writers and among the most compassionate, among the most in touch with people's aspirations for a better future.

Notes to Part 1

1. Because Kate Chopin's career was short and because some of her stories were published years after she wrote them—and some were not published at all in her lifetime—the date included in parentheses after each short story in this volume is the year of composition. Exact dates of composition and publication for Chopin's stories can be found at the end of Per Seyersted's *Complete Works of Kate Chopin* and in Per Seyersted and Emily Toth, eds., *A Kate Chopin Miscellany* (Natchitoches, LA: Northwestern State University Press, 1979). The year in parentheses after *books*—Chopin's or others'—is the publication date.

2. Thirty years ago, discussing *The Awakening*, Stanley Kauffmann wrote that "Kate Chopin was at least a generation ahead of her time," that her novel was "an anachronistic, lonely, existentialist voice out of the mid-20th century." "The Really Lost Generation," *The New Republic* 3 December 1966, 38. Were he writing today, Kauffmann might well say the late twentieth century.

3. Kenneth E. Eble, "Review of Per Seyersted, *Kate Chopin: A Critical Biography* and *The Complete Works of Kate Chopin*," *American Literary Realism* 4 (1971):83.

4. Daniel Aaron, "Per Seyersted: *Kate Chopin: A Critical Biography*," *Edda* 71 (1971):342; hereafter cited in the text.

5. George Arms, "Kate Chopin's *The Awakening* in the Perspective of her Literary Career," *Essays on American Literature in Honor of Jay B. Hubbell*, ed. Clarence Gohdes (Durham, NC: Duke University Press, 1967), 222; hereafter cited in the text.

6. Chopin had sent most of the stories she included in her two published volumes, and most of those she scheduled for *A Vocation and a Voice*, to magazines as she wrote them, and many appeared in magazines before being reprinted or scheduled for reprinting in her collections.

7. See Charles J. Stivale, *The Art of Rupture: Narrative Desire and Duplicity in the Tales of Guy de Maupassant* (Ann Arbor: University of Michigan Press, 1994); Mary Donaldson-Evans, *A Woman's Revenge: The Chronology of Dispossession in Maupassant's Fiction* (Lexington, KY: French Forum, 1986); and A. H. Wallace, *Guy de Maupassant* (New York: Twayne, 1973).

8. Henry James, *Partial Portraits*. 1888 (Westport, CT: Greenwood, 1970), 249; hereafter cited in the text.

9. See Graham King, *Garden of Zola: Emile Zola and His Novels for English Readers* (New York: Harper & Row, 1978); David F. Bell, *Models of Power: Politics and Economics in Zola's Rougon-Macquart* (Lincoln: University of Nebraska Press, 1988); and Ernest Alfred Vizetelly, *Émile Zola: An Account of His Life and Work* (London: John Lane, Bodley Head, 1904).

10. See Edith Harding and Philip Riley, *The Bilingual Family* (New York: Cambridge University Press, 1986) and E. de Jong, *The Bilingual Experience* (New York: Cambridge University Press, 1986).

11. William Hyde and Howard L. Conrad, eds., *Encyclopedia of the History of St. Louis,* (New York: Southern History, 1899) 1, 358.

12. See also Jean Bardot, *L'Influence Française dans la Vie et L'Œuvre de Kate Chopin.* (Thèse de Doctorat, Université de Paris-IV, 1985–86).

13. Edmund Wilson, foreword to *The Complete Works of Kate Chopin,* ed. Per Seyersted, 2 vols. (Baton Rouge: Louisiana State University Press, 1969), 1:14.

14. Chopin says that she writes by instinct, that "story-writing—at least with me—is the spontaneous expression of impressions gathered goodness knows where" (722). Winfried Fluck notes that "The Story of an Hour" is a good example of "the ways in which conflicting impulses shape the logic and movement" of Chopin's stories. "Tentative Transgressions: Kate Chopin's Fiction as a Mode of Symbolic Action," *Studies in American Fiction* 10 (1982):154.

15. Francis A. Walker, *Statistical Atlas of the United States Based on the Results of the 9th Census, 1870* (Washington: Congress of the United States, 1874). See Plates XXIII, XXIV, XXVI, and XXXIX. Some scholars are uncertain about the accuracy of the 1870 census, especially in the South, because of lingering effects of the Civil War. See also Stephan Thernstrom, ed., *Harvard Encyclopedia of American Ethnic Groups* (Cambridge: Belknap, 1980), 1047–52.

16. John Seelye, ed., *The Adventures of Huckleberry Finn by Mark Twain,* 1885 (New York: Penguin, 1986), xxxii.

17. Louisiana African Americans descended from the servants of the Creoles sometimes call themselves Creoles or are called that by others. See Gary B. Mills, *The Forgotten People: Cane River's Creoles of Color* (Baton Rouge: Louisiana State University Press, 1977), and Arnold R. Hirsch and Joseph Logsdon, eds., *Creole New Orleans: Race and Americanization* (Baton Rouge: Louisiana State University Press, 1992).

18. Larzer Ziff, *The American 1890s: Life and Times of a Lost Generation* (New York: Viking, 1966), 297.

19. See Carl A. Brasseaux, *Acadian to Cajun: Transformation of a People, 1803–1877* (Jackson: University Press of Mississippi, 1992).

20. Nina Baym, ed., *The Awakening and Selected Short Stories by Kate Chopin* (New York: Modern Library, 1981), xx.

21. "Struggles over ethnic or regional identity—in other words, over the properties (stigmata or emblems) linked with the *origin* through the *place* of origin and its associated durable marks, such as accent—are a particular case of the different struggles over classifications, struggles over the monopoly of the power to make people see and believe, to get them to know and recognize, to impose the legitimate definition of the divisions of the social world and, thereby, to *make and unmake groups.* What is at stake here is the power of imposing a vision of the social world through principles of di-vision which, when they are imposed on a whole group, establish meaning and a consensus about meaning, and in particular about the identity and unity of the group, which creates the reality of the unity and the identity of the group." Pierre Bourdieu, *Language and Symbolic*

Power, trans. Gino Raymond and Matthew Adamson (Cambridge: Harvard University Press, 1991), 221. See also Bourdieu's *The Field of Cultural Production: Essays on Art and Literature* (New York: Columbia University Press, 1993) and *Distinction: A Social Critique of the Judgement of Taste,* trans. Richard Nice (Cambridge: Harvard University Press, 1984).

22. Chopin had written a sketch, "Emancipation: A Life Fable," when she was 19. She had begun "A No-Account Creole" in 1888 and written four or five other stories before she finished it in 1891.

23. Chopin's use of an outsider in this story and many others may have been influenced by the work of George Sand. See Nancy E. Rogers, "Echoes of George Sand in Kate Chopin," *Revue de Littérature Comparée* 1 (1983):39–40; hereafter cited in the text.

24. Emily Toth argues that Alcée Laballière in "At the 'Cadian Ball" is modeled after a man with whom Kate Chopin had a romance during her Natchitoches years (Toth, 212).

25. Barbara Ewell complains about the "manipulative and class-conscious pairings" in "At the 'Cadian Ball" in her study *Kate Chopin* (New York: Ungar, 1986), 171; hereafter cited in the text. But it is people's striving to prosper within the restraints created by such cultural dispositions that constitutes the heart of some of Kate Chopin's best fiction.

26. "At the 'Cadian Ball" was the first Kate Chopin story to be reprinted in an anthology. Robert L. Ramsay included it in *Short Stories of America* in 1921, because, he argues, Chopin captures "a civilization quite unlike anything else America can show," offering a "local color of Social Heritage" dependent on traditions and history. He finds in "At the 'Cadian Ball" a complex plot with two interwoven parts, each "simple, comic, and accelerated," and he guides readers to examine its "grouping" of characters and its "almost exclusively direct" characterization, its "finished" use of dialect, its "various kinds of sentiment," its "angle of narration," and its "indirect" ending. Robert L. Ramsay, ed., *Short Stories of America* (Boston: Houghton Mifflin, 1921), 14, 22, 324–38. For a description of which Chopin stories have been anthologized when and where, see Bernard Koloski, "The Anthologized Chopin: Kate Chopin's Short Stories in Yesterday's and Today's Anthologies," *Louisiana Literature* 11 (1994):18–30; hereafter cited in the text.

27. Richard H. Potter, "Negroes in the Fiction of Kate Chopin," *Louisiana History* 12 (1971):47; hereafter cited in the text.

28. Quoted by Per Seyersted in *Kate Chopin: A Critical Biography* (Baton Rouge: Louisiana State University Press, 1969), 186; hereafter cited in the text.

29. Fred Lewis Pattee, *The Development of the American Short Story: An Historical Survey* (New York: Harper, 1923), 327.

30. Arthur Hobson Quinn, *American Fiction: An Historical and Critical Survey* (New York: Appleton-Century, 1936), 355.

31. In a children's story, "Beyond the Bayou," Chopin presents a woman who does cross an imaginary boundary, with salutary effects.

32. Anna Shannon Elfenbein, *Women on the Color Line: Evolving Stereotypes and the Writings of George Washington Cable, Grace King, and Kate Chopin* (Charlottesville: University Press of Virginia, 1989), 134; hereafter cited in the text.

33. Patricia Hopkins Lattin, "Kate Chopin's Repeating Characters," *Mississippi Quarterly* 33 (1980):30.

34. See Stephan Thernstrom, ed., *Harvard Encyclopedia of American Ethnic Groups* (Cambridge: Belknap, 1980), 380–81, 1047–52.

35. See Werner Sollors, *Beyond Ethnicity: Consent and Descent in American Culture* (New York: Oxford University Press, 1986), 212–21; hereafter cited in the text.

36. See Bernard Koloski, "The Swinburne Lines in *The Awakening*," *American Literature* 45 (1974):608–10.

37. Allen F. Stein, *After the Vows Were Spoken: Marriage in American Literary Realism* (Columbus: Ohio State University Press, 1984), 191; hereafter cited in the text.

38. See section 21 of the 1892 edition of *Leaves of Grass*.

39. Howe is describing characters in nineteenth-century Russian fiction. Irving Howe, *A Critic's Notebook* (New York: Harcourt Brace, 1994), 55.

40. Helen Taylor, *Gender, Race, and Region in the Writings of Grace King, Ruth McEnery Stuart, and Kate Chopin* (Baton Rouge: Louisiana State University Press, 1989), xiii; hereafter cited in the text.

41. In an earlier essay, Taylor had seen the matter differently. "In all Kate Chopin's stories," she wrote seven years before the publication of her recent book, "the three racial groups ['the Creoles, the French Acadians and the Negroes of Louisiana'] share many qualities; all three are seen as easygoing, hedonistic and high spirited; all are superstitious, passionate and volatile. The contrasts and relationships between the three cultures provide much of the humour, as well as the dramatic and ironic tension throughout her work." Helen Taylor, ed., *Kate Chopin Portraits* (London: Women's Press, 1982), xiv. In spite of her intention in her recent book to pursue "close readings of the texts themselves" (Taylor, xiii), Taylor does not discuss in any detail any of the Chopin short stories that lead her to her new conclusions about race.

42. Toni Morrison, *Playing in the Dark: Whiteness and the Literary Imagination* (Cambridge: Harvard University Press, 1992), xii–xiii.

43. Per Seyersted describes ways that "Regret" resembles a story by Guy de Maupassant (Seyersted, 125–30).

44. Birds in cages, for example, are present in both "At Chênière Caminada" and *The Awakening*. See the first page of the novel and p. 317 of the story. Helen Taylor notes that Chopin's New Orleans contemporary Grace King had published a story with the same title a few months before Chopin published hers (Taylor, 174).

45. Chopin changed the ending of this story at the suggestion of the editor of the *Century* (Toth 283). In her earlier version she apparently had Telèsphore marry Zaïda.

46. A recent translation of *A Vocation and a Voice* into French is called *La Cigarette Égyptienne*, after "An Egyptian Cigarette," one of the stories in the volume. The translator gives no explanation for the title change. *La Cigarette Égyptienne*, trans. Marie-Claude Peugeot (Paris: Anatolia, 1995).

47. For a discussion of Suzima's voice, see Bert Bender, "Kate Chopin's Lyrical Short Stories," *Studies in Short Fiction* 11 (1974):261.

48. Daniel Rankin, *Kate Chopin and Her Creole Stories* (Philadelphia: University of Pennsylvania Press, 1932), 48, 144.

49. Opera music was available for piano, so Kate Chopin, who occasionally composed music for the piano, may have played some of it.

50. The twins bear the same name as Adrienne Farival of "Lilacs."

51. Hérold left *Ludovic* unfinished. It was completed after his death by F. Halévy. The words are by J. H. Vernoy de Saint-Georges. I am grateful to Sion M. Honea of the Sibley Music Library at the Eastman School of Music in Rochester, New York, for making available the vocal score of the opera and to staff of the Bibliothèque Municipale de Toulouse, in France, for making available the full opera.

52. The woman eventually asks her cousin to persuade the army not to shoot Ludovic.

53. Gerda Taranow, *Sarah Bernhardt: The Art Within the Legend* (Princeton: Princeton University Press, 1972), 109; hereafter cited in the text. See also Eric Salmon, ed., *Bernhardt and the Theatre of Her Time* (Westport: Greenwood, 1984); Cornelia Otis Skinner, *Madame Sarah* (Boston: Houghton Mifflin, 1966); and Arthur Gold and Robert Fizdale, *The Divine Sarah: A Life of Sarah Bernhardt* (New York: Alfred A. Knopf, 1991).

54. Angus Wilson, *Emile Zola: An Introductory Study of His Novels* (New York: Morrow, 1952), 46.

55. Victorien Sardou, *Théâtre Complet*, Tome I (Paris: Editions Albin Michel, 1934), 383–538. The play was first performed in Paris in 1882 with Bernhardt in the title role. The opera, *Fedora*, by Giordano Umberto—based on Sardou's play—was composed a few years after Kate Chopin wrote her short story.

56. Chopin published "The Falling in Love of Fedora" under a pen name, "La Tour," "the tower." The masculine French "le tour" carries the same meaning as English "the tour," though a French actress or other traveling artist would conduct "la tournée."

57. Joyce Dyer, "The Restive Brute: The Symbolic Presentation of Repression and Sublimation in Kate Chopin's 'Fedora,' " *Studies in Short Fiction* 18 (1981):261–65. Dyer mentions Sardou's play.

58. Susan Koppelman, ed., *Two Friends and Other Nineteenth-Century Lesbian Stories by American Women Writers* (New York: Meridian, 1994), 177.

59. Peggy Skaggs has traced the implications of this phrase through several Chopin short stories. See " 'The Man-Instinct of Possession': A Persistent Theme in Kate Chopin's Stories," *Louisiana Studies* 14 (1975):277–85.

60. Allen Stein finds a "virulent hostility" in the actions of the woman in "Her Letters" (Stein, 187).

61. Patricia Hopkins Lattin describes this story as one of several that "involves characters, who, clearly incomplete and out of touch with themselves, are also isolated from their fellow human beings and must reestablish human contact before they can find themselves." "The Search for Self in Kate Chopin's Fiction: Simple Versus Complex Vision," *Southern Studies* 21 (1982):223.

62. None of the principal characters in "Beyond the Bayou" is referred to by his or her given name.

63. "Beyond the Bayou" helps bring into focus a current connecting *Bayou Folk* and *A Night in Acadie*. People break out of personally and culturally constructed dreams or boundaries when the well-being of someone they love is threatened. Placide in "A No-Account Creole" gives up his claim to marry Euphrasie when he finds her heart set upon someone else. Ma'ame Pélagie abandons her dream of a reconstructed manor house when she sees her sister in agony because La Petite may leave. The subject appears again in "A Matter of Prejudice" and other *A Night in Acadie* stories.

64. See Koloski, 27–28.

65. See Philippe Ariès, *Centuries of Childhood: A Social History of Family Life* (New York: Alfred A. Knopf, 1962), 412.

66. Per Seyersted includes in the second volume of Chopin's *Complete Works* and in *A Kate Chopin Miscellany* a listing of where Chopin's stories were published. Emily Toth describes in her biography where Chopin submitted her stories and which were not published after being accepted. Toth also lists several stories she considers to have been written for a children's audience. I include those stories in my count of children's stories here, though it seems to me that some other stories might well be thought of as being directed to children and that some published in children's magazines speak powerfully to adults as much as to children. According to Seyersted's and Toth's listings and descriptions, these, in order of composition, are Chopin's children's stories: "For Marse Chouchoute," "The Maid of Saint Phillippe," "A Wizard from Gettysburg," "A Rude Awakening," "A Very Fine Fiddle," "Boulôt and Boulotte," "Love on the Bon-Dieu," "Beyond the Bayou," "After the Winter," "The Bênitous' Slave," "A Turkey Hunt," "Old Aunt Peggy," "The Lilies," "Ripe Figs," "Croque-Mitaine," "A Little Free-Mulatto," "Loka," "Mamouche," "A Matter of Prejudice," "Polydore," "Madame Martel's Christmas Eve," "Aunt Lympy's Interference," "Ti Frère," "A Horse Story," "A Little Country Girl," "Alexandre's Wonderful Experience," "A December Day in Dixie," "The Gentleman from New Orleans," "Charlie," "The Wood-Choppers," and "Polly."

67. See Peter Hunt, *An Introduction to Children's Literature* (New York: Oxford University Press, 1994), 1–26, 163–83; hereafter cited in the text.

68. Perry Nodelman, "Interpretation and the Apparent Sameness of Children's Novels," *Studies in the Literary Imagination* 18 (1985):20.

69. See, however, Peggy Skaggs's essay in Part 3 of this volume.

70. Joyce Carol Oates, ed., *The Oxford Book of American Short Stories* (New York: Oxford University Press, 1992), 129.

71. "The Storm" has, like *The Awakening*, become almost obligatory reading for many American university students. College textbook editors, however, and editors of collections of short stories by multiple authors almost always reprint "The Storm" without its subtitle, "A Sequel to 'The 'Cadian Ball,' " and they do not reprint the earlier story. Editors of anthologies of short stories by Kate Chopin alone always include both stories (see Koloski, 26). Kate Chopin did not mean for "The Storm" to be read by itself. The story does not yield its full power apart from "At the 'Cadian Ball."

72. Anna Shannon Elfenbein links Calixta in "The Storm" with the "dark women" in "Désirée's Baby" and "La Belle Zoraïde," incorporating the three stories into a discussion of the way in which the antebellum stereotype of the "tragic octoroon" is present in the fiction of Kate Chopin. She argues that Calixta "enjoys an easy sexuality denied to white women" and that "because of her presumed racial difference, Calixta experiences her sexuality fully." Kate Chopin, Elfenbein says, "hedges" her "implicit criticism of bourgeois marriage" by "imputing passion to a woman already degraded in the popular imagination, exploiting rather than challenging conventional prejudices" (Elfenbein, 135). Readers should note that while Calixta shares some characteristics with other "dark" women in Chopin's work, she has no black blood. Everybody in "At the 'Cadian Ball" and "The Storm" understands her to be white.

73. After discussing *The Awakening* and "The Storm," Allen F. Stein concludes: "Though it is clear that Chopin has it in mind to assert the unique worth of each individual in the face of the restraints and repressions of convention, the effect of her work is invariably to do otherwise. Instead of a world in which people and the choices they make matter, she presents a bleak scene in which they bounce off one another chaotically in unending, unthinking response to impulses over which they have no control and little understanding. Nor does she maintain the ethical framework that redeems from moral chaos those essays by Emerson such as 'Experience,' 'Fate,' and 'Power' of which her work is in its emphasis on the deterministically ordered pursuit of self-fulfillment more than a little reminiscent. Her very insistence that moral questions are irrelevant to the ways in which people live undercuts her obvious effort to point up that individuals count for something and makes for an implicit condescension to her characters and their dreams that comes through in everything she wrote. No intellectual, apparently unable or unwilling to think her impressions through, Chopin, in spite of herself, presents in her pieces on married men and women as bleak a picture of the human conditions as one can find in late-nineteenth-century American writing" (Stein, 206–7).

74. At 13,600 words, "Charlie" is about a thousand words longer than "Athénaïse," which is about a thousand words longer than "A Vocation and a

Voice." Chopin would write only five stories—three of them for children—after "Charlie," two more in 1900 and one each year for the following three years.

75. Anne M. Blythe, "Kate Chopin's 'Charlie,' " *Kate Chopin Reconsidered: Beyond the Bayou,* ed. Lynda S. Boren and Sara deSaussure Davis (Baton Rouge: Louisiana State University Press, 1992), 207.

76. Barbara Ewell says "Charlie" represents a "compromise of love and independence," a sign that Chopin's "courage was failing." Chopin could not, she argues, "imagine a fictional equivalent for the independent female within the structures of marriage" (Ewell, 179–80). Emily Toth reads the story as a "retreat" for Chopin "into material from her Sacred Heart past" (Toth, 377). But Judie Newman argues that Charlie "transcends the script offered by her culture" and backs her position by exploring at length Chopin's "complex of images associated with the hand." "Kate Chopin: Short Fiction and the Arts of Subversion," *The Nineteenth-Century American Short Story,* ed. A. Robert Lee (New York: Vision, 1985), 154.

77. She apparently destroyed a novel called *Young Dr. Gosse.*

78. A few critics today argue strongly in behalf of stories not discussed in this volume. See especially the work of Joyce Dyer, listed in the bibliography. Also see note 46.

79. See the bibliography at the close of this volume.

80. Elaine Showalter, "Chopin and American Women Writers," *Kate Chopin, The Awakening* ed. Margo Culley, 2d ed. (New York: Norton, 1994), 319.

81. See Loïc J. D. Wacquant, preface to *An Invitation to Reflexive Sociology,* by Pierre Bourdieu and Loïc J. D. Wacquant (Chicago: University of Chicago Press, 1992), 19–26.

Part 2

THE WRITER

Introduction

Only after she had completed a novel, half her stories, and a short-story anthology did Kate Chopin begin to publish her views of literature. Though she had read widely throughout her life, she was reluctant to present herself as critic. When she did, it was with bold convictions about what literature should or should not be.

She objects to the "provincialism" she finds in members of the Western Association of Writers who celebrate the beauty of life in the country or faith in a God who "manifests himself through the sectional church." She is unhappy with Hamlin Garland's refusal, one common among American realists at the time, to treat "such primitive passions as love, hate, etc." She quotes Garland's argument that "in real life people do not talk love." She is contemptuous of it. "How does he know?" she demands. "I feel very sorry for Mr. Garland" (691–94).

Emile Zola's *Lourdes,* she writes, is a "mistake," but not a "failure" (697), and Thomas Hardy's *Jude the Obscure* "has the outward appearance of a Congressional Record" (713). But for her beloved Guy de Maupassant she has nothing but praise.

When pressed into talking about herself, she warns that she once took a vow to "never be confidential except for the purpose of misleading" (700), but she then goes on to describe with candor her belief in using her own "faculty" (704), whatever it may be, and documents in detail when, where, and why she writes. "Story-writing," she says, "—at least with me—is the spontaneous expression of impressions gathered goodness knows where. To seek the source, the impulse of a story is like tearing a flower to pieces for wantonness" (722).

Unlike her contemporary Henry James, Kate Chopin does not take well to writing literary criticism. And she does not like to speak of herself or her family. "The *real* Edwin Booth," she says about one of the great actors of her time, "gave himself to his public through his art" (695), not through his private letters. She herself has done the same. "My latest book?" she asks. "Why, you will find it, no doubt, at the bookseller's or the libraries" (722).

The Western Association of Writers

Provincialism in the best sense of the word stamps the character of this association of writers, who gather chiefly from the State of Indiana and meet annually at Spring Fountain Park. It is an ideally beautiful spot, a veritable garden of Eden in which the disturbing fruit of the tree of knowledge still hangs unplucked. The cry of the dying century has not reached this body of workers, or else it has not been comprehended. There is no doubt in their souls, no unrest: apparently an abiding faith in God as he manifests himself through the sectional church, and an overmastering love of their soil and institutions.

Most of them are singers. Their native streams, trees, bushes and birds, the lovely country life about them, form the chief burden of their often too sentimental songs.

Occasionally the voice of one of them reaches out across the prairies and is heard by the world beyond. For this is the soil, these are the conditions, and the Western Association of Writers are the typical human group which have given us James Whitcomb Riley, Mrs. Catherwood and Lew Wallace.

Among these people are to be found an earnestness in the acquirement and dissemination of book-learning, a clinging to past and conventional standards, an almost Creolean sensitiveness to criticism and a singular ignorance of, or disregard for, the value of the highest art forms.

There is a very, very big world lying not wholly in northern Indiana, nor does it lie at the antipodes, either. It is human existence in its subtle, complex, true meaning, stripped of the veil with which ethical and conventional standards have draped it. When the Western Association of Writers with their earnestness of purpose and poetic insights shall have developed into students of true life and true art, who knows but they may produce a genius such as America has not yet known.

Published in *The Critic* on 7 July 1894.

"Crumbling Idols" by Hamlin Garland

Mr. Garland seems not content that the idols whereof he speaks are crumbling. He attempts to hasten their demolition with hammer-strokes that resound and make much noise, even if they accomplish nothing in that work of destruction which moves too slowly for his impatient humor.

In these twelve essays on art, however, the author has sounded a true note if not a new one, which would be more forcible were it less insistent; which would ring clearer were it not accompanied by a clamor and bluster often distressing to sensitive ears. He suggests—what no one who has thought upon the subject is ready to dispute—that the youthful artist should free himself from the hold of conventionalism; that he should go direct to those puissant sources, Life and Nature, for inspiration and turn his back upon models furnished by man; in a word, that he should be creative and not imitative. But Mr. Garland undervalues the importance of the past in art and exaggerates the significance of the present.

Human impulses do not change and can not so long as men and women continue to stand in the relation to one another which they have occupied since our knowledge of their existence began. It is why Æschylus is true, and Shakespeare is true to-day, and why Ibsen will not be true in some remote to-morrow, however forcible and representative he may be for the hour, because he takes for his themes social problems which by their very nature are mutable. And, notwithstanding Mr. Garland's opinion to the contrary, social problems, social environments, local color and the rest of it are not *of themselves* motives to insure the survival of a writer who employs them.

The author of "Crumbling Idols" would even lightly dismiss from the artist's consideration such primitive passions as love, hate, etc. He declares that in real life people do not talk love. How does he know? I feel very sorry for Mr. Garland.

Published in *St. Louis Life* on 6 October 1894.

Part 2

An excellent chapter in the book deals with impressionism in painting. It will be found interesting and even instructive to many who have rather vague and confused notions of what impressionism means. Mr. Garland has gone over heart and soul to the Impressionists. He feels and sees with them; being in close sympathy with their individualism; their abandonment of the traditional and conventional in the interest of "truth." He admits that he himself has discovered certain "purple shadows" by looking at a stretch of sand, with his head turned top-side down! It is doubtful if many of us would exhibit an equal zeal in pursuing anything so elusive as a shadow; but the incident goes to prove Mr. Garland's earnestness and sincerity of purpose.

His attitude in regard to the East as a literary center is to be deplored; and his expressions in that respect seem exaggerated and uncalled for. The fact remains that Chicago is not yet a literary center, nor is St. Louis (!), nor San Francisco, nor Denver, nor any of those towns in whose behalf he drops into prophecy. There can no good come of abusing Boston and New York. On the contrary, as "literary centers" they have rendered incalculable service to the reading world by bringing to light whatever there has been produced of force and originality in the West and South since the war.

The book is one which all Western art lovers should read. Mr. Garland is surely a representative Western man of letters. He is too young to assume the role of prophet becomingly; and he somehow gives the impression of a man who has not yet "lived," but he is vigorous and sincere, and he is one of us.

The Real Edwin Booth

The October *Century* opens with a selection of private letters of the late Edwin Booth, preceded by a brief preface from his daughter, Mrs. Grossman. The article bears the title, "The Real Edwin Booth," and forms part of a collection to be published later in book form.

If Booth were able to-day to take up the magazine and re-read these letters, never intended for the public eye, it is easy to fancy him quoting from one of them, "I shrink from the indelicacy."

Never has the world known a man more wrapped about in a mantle of sensitiveness and reserve than was Edwin Booth; and it seems a pity that in his case the public might not have respected the mute appeal for privacy which his whole existence expressed.

Judging from the selection before us one can hardly hope that these letters will throw any new light upon the man's relation to his life work—which could give some excuse for their being, so far as the public is concerned. They simply show us a man who seems fond of his daughter and of his friends; they lay bare the poignant sorrow of a husband for the loss of a well-beloved wife; they indicate that he possessed some heart, so far as the written word can represent so abstract a thing as a human heart; and they evince little or no power of mind or depth of character. No, it is not here that we are to look for the real Edwin Booth, in a puerile collection of letters, expressions wrung from him by the conventional demands of his daily life.

The *real* Edwin Booth gave himself to the public through his art. Those of us who most felt its magnetic power are the ones who knew him best, and as he would have wished to be known. His art was his closest and most precious possession. Through it he was great, he was individual, he was a force that appealed to and acted upon the finer responsive chords of every human intelligence that heard him. It was the medium through which he expressed himself. He possessed no other form of expression by which to make himself known.

Published in *St. Louis Life* on 13 October 1894.

Part 2

If he might to-day turn over the leaves of this collection of letters, it would surely be with that sad, "pale smile" which we all remember, and no doubt with a spoken reproach to all of us—public, daughter and publishers: "Why look you, how unworthy a thing you make of me."

Emile Zola's "Lourdes"

I once heard a devotee of impressionism admit, in looking at a picture by Monet, that, while he himself had never seen in nature the peculiar yellows and reds therein depicted, he was convinced that Monet had painted them because he saw them and because they were true. With something of a kindred faith in the sincerity of all Mons. Zola's work, I am yet not at all times ready to admit its truth, which is only equivalent to saying that our points of view differ, that truth rests upon a shifting basis and is apt to be kaleidoscopic.

"Lourdes" seems to me to be a mistake, not in its conception, but in its treatment. It cannot be called a failure, because Mons. Zola has not failed in his intention to give to the world an exhaustive history of Bernadette's Lourdes. But that history could have been as direct, and surely more effective, had it been made subordinate to some powerful narrative, such as Mons. Zola is so well able to invent.

As it is, the story is the merest thread of a story running loosely through the 400 pages, and more than two-thirds of the time swamped beneath a mass of prosaic data, offensive and nauseous description and rampant sentimentality.

In no former work has Mons. Zola so glaringly revealed his constructive methods. Not for an instant, from first to last, do we lose sight of the author and his note-book and of the disagreeable fact that his design is to instruct us. Pierre, the hero of the book, seems to be also the victim, the passive medium chosen by the author to convey information to his readers. This young man (an unbeliever) is inspired with an inordinate tenderness for the memory of Bernadette, solely that he may chance to be carrying her history in his coat pocket that he may read it to the pilgrims journeying on the "white train" towards Lourdes, and that the reader may in this way become acquainted with it himself. Once at Lourdes, the movements of this young priest come to be looked upon by the reader with uneasiness and misgiving. If he happen to walk abroad, we need not suppose it is to take the air, or that it is for

Published in *St. Louis Life* on 17 November 1894.

any other purpose than to be waylaid by one of the many individuals who seem to swarm in Lourdes, ever on the watch for willing ears in which to empty the overflowing vials of their information. If he sits for a moment contemplative before the Grotto, the insidious man of knowledge is soon there beside him, conveying to him by pages and pages information which we know that Mons. Zola acquired in the same way and thus subtly conveys to us.

We are told that Pierre goes to the barber's to be shaved, but we know better by this time; we know that he goes for some other purpose, which soon reveals itself when the intelligent barber tells in round terms what he thinks of certain clerical abuses prevailing at Lourdes, and we are certain that we are hearing what the author himself thinks of those things. Such handling of a subject is unpardonable in Mons. Zola.

The style all through, however, is masterly, and there are descriptive bits which are superb, notably the description of a candle-light procession winding its tortuous way in and out among the hills: "Au ciel il semblait y avoir moins d'étoiles. Une voie lactée était tombée de la haut roulant son pondroiement de mondes, et qui continuait sur la terre la ronde des astres."

Very powerfully conceived and described is the scene before the Grotto, leading up to Marie Guersaint's remarkable cure. The writer here touches a fine psychological point, though not a new one—the possibility of the combined will-power of a mass of humanity forcing nature to subserve its ends. A French savant has already reminded us that "the psychology of a multitude of men is not the psychology of the individual." The subject is attractive, and Mons. Zola might have made more of it.

"Lourdes" has been roundly denounced by Catholics and, I think, the ban of the Church set upon it. I cannot see why. It is a book which I think a good Catholic would greatly enjoy reading, the only and easy condition being to set aside Mons. Zola's point of view and color his facts with one's own. He has a thorough knowledge of Catholicism, extending to the most trifling mannerisms of its votaries, and this part of his subject he handles delicately and captivatingly.

But the book will doubtless thrust him a step further away from the goal of his hopes and ambitions—the French Academy.

It is hard to understand in Mons. Zola this persistent desire to be admitted to the Academy. One would suppose he would be content, even proud, to stand outside of its doors in the company of Alphonse Daudet.

From "Confidences"

About eight years ago there fell accidentally into my hands a volume of Maupassant's tales. These were new to me. I had been in the woods, in the fields, groping around; looking for something big, satisfying, convincing, and finding nothing but—myself; a something neither big nor satisfying but wholly convincing. It was at this period of my emerging from the vast solitude in which I had been making my own acquaintance, that I stumbled upon Maupassant. I read his stories and marvelled at them. Here was life, not fiction; for where were the plots, the old fashioned mechanism and stage trapping that in a vague, unthinking way I had fancied were essential to the art of story making. Here was a man who had escaped from tradition and authority, who had entered into himself and looked out upon life through his own being and with his own eyes; and who, in a direct and simple way, told us what he saw. When a man does this, he gives us the best that he can; something valuable for it is genuine and spontaneous. He gives us his impressions. Some one told me the other day that Maupassant had gone out of fashion. I was not grieved to hear it. He has never seemed to me to belong to the multitude, but rather to the individual. He is not one whom we gather in crowds to listen to—whom we follow in procession—with beating of brass instruments. He does not move us to throw ourselves into the throng—having the integral of an unthinking whole to shout his praise. I even like to think that he appeals to me alone. You probably like to think that he reaches you exclusively. A whole multitude may be secretly nourishing the belief in regard to him for all I know. Someway I like to cherish the delusion that he has spoken to no one else so directly, so intimately as he does to me. He did not say, as another might have done, "do you see these are charming stories of mine? take them into your closet—study them closely—mark their combination—observe the method, the manner of their putting together—and if ever you are moved to write stories you can do no better than to imitate . . .

In the Confidence of a Story-Writer

There is registered somewhere in my consciousness a vow that I will never be confidential except for the purpose of misleading. But consistency is a pompous and wearisome burden, and I seek relief by casting it aside; for, like the colored gentleman in the Passemala, I am sometimes "afraid o' myse'f," but never ashamed.

I have discovered my limitations, and I have saved myself much worry and torment by accepting them as final. I can gain nothing but tribulation by cultivating faculties that are not my own. I cannot reach anything by running after it, but I find that many pleasant and profitable things come to me here in my corner.

Some wise man has promulgated an eleventh commandment, "Thou shalt not preach," which, interpreted, means, "Thou shalt not instruct thy neighbor as to what he should do." But the Preacher is always with us. Said one to me: "Thou shalt parcel off thy day into mathematical sections. So many hours shalt thou abandon thyself to thought, so many to writing; a certain number shalt thou devote to household duties, to social enjoyment, to ministering to thy afflicted fellow creatures." I listened to the voice of the Preacher, and the result was stagnation all along the line of "hours" and unspeakable bitterness of spirit. In brutal revolt I turned to and played solitaire during my "thinking hour," and whist when I should have been ministering to the afflicted. I scribbled a little during my "social enjoyment" period, and shattered the "household duties" into fragments of every conceivable fraction of time, with which I besprinkled the entire day as from a pepper-box. In this way I succeeded in reëstablishing the harmonious discord and confusion which had surrounded me before I listened to the voice, and which seems necessary to my physical and mental well-being.

But there are many voices preaching. Said another one to me: "Go forth and gather wisdom in the intellectual atmosphere of clubs,—in those centres of thought where questions are debated and knowledge is disseminated." Once more giving heed, I hurried to enroll myself among

Published in *Atlantic Monthly* in January 1899.

the thinkers, and dispensers of knowledge, and propounders of questions. And very much out of place did I feel in these intellectual gatherings. I escaped by some pretext, and regained my corner, where no "questions" and no fine language can reach me.

There is far too much gratuitous advice bandied about, regardless of personal aptitude and wholly confusing to the individual point of view.

I had heard so often reiterated that "genius is a capacity for taking pains" that the axiom had become lodged in my brain with the fixedness of a fundamental truth. I had never hoped or aspired to be a genius. But one day the thought occurred to me, "I will take pains." Thereupon I proceeded to lie awake at night plotting a tale that should convince my limited circle of readers that I could rise above the commonplace. As to choice of "time," the present century offered too prosaic a setting for a tale intended to stir the heart and the imagination. I selected the last century. It is true I know little of the last century, and have a feeble imagination. I read volumes bearing upon the history of the times and people that I proposed to manipulate, and pored over folios depicting costumes and household utensils then in use, determined to avoid inaccuracy. For the first time in my life I took notes,—copious notes,—and carried them bulging in my jacket pockets, until I felt as if I were wearing Zola's coat. I have never seen a craftsman at work upon a fine piece of mosaic, but I fancy that he must handle the delicate bits much as I handled the words in that story, picking, selecting, grouping, with an eye to color and to artistic effect,—never satisfied. The story completed, I was very, very weary; but I had the satisfaction of feeling that for once in my life I had worked hard, I had achieved something great, I had taken pains.

But the story failed to arouse enthusiasm among the editors. It is at present lying in my desk. Even my best friend declined to listen to it, when I offered to read it to her.

I am more than ever convinced that a writer should be content to use his own faculty, whether it be a faculty for taking pains or a faculty for reaching his effects by the most careless methods. Every writer, I fancy, has his group of readers who understand, who are in sympathy with his thoughts or impressions or whatever he gives them. And he who is content to reach his own group, without ambition to be heard beyond it, attains, in my opinion, somewhat to the dignity of a philosopher.

From "As You Like It," Part IV

A while ago there was lying upon my table a book, which for some inscrutable reason has been withdrawn, I am told, from circulation at our libraries. The spectacle of this book lying in evidence communicated a severe shock to the susceptibilities of a woman who was calling upon me.

"Oh! how can you!" she exclaimed, "with so many young people about!"

The question of how much or how little knowledge of life should be withheld from the youthful mind is one which need only be touched upon here. It is a subject about which there exists a diversity of opinion with the conservative element no doubt, greatly in preponderance. As a rule the youthful, untrained nature is left to gather wisdom as it comes along in a thousand-and-one ways and in whatever form it may present itself to the intelligent, the susceptible, the observant. In this respect experience is perhaps an abler instructor than direct enlightenment from man or woman; for it works by suggestion. There are many phases and features of life which cannot, or rather should not be expounded, demonstrated, presented to the youthful imagination as cold facts, for it is safe to assert they are not going to be accepted as such. It is moreover robbing youth of its privilege to gather wisdom as the bee gathers honey.

The book referred to a moment ago is a ponderous and formidable looking affair at best. There is nothing alluring in its title or in its sombre black binding. It has the outward appearance of a Congressional Record, and it might easily have escaped the attention of the young person if some reviewers, a few gossips and the libraries had seen fit to let it work out its own damnation. I read the book and then I laid it upon the table.

"Any good?" asked one or two youngsters who have a propensity for getting at the inside of an interesting novel.

"Unutterably tiresome," I said, "but you might like it."

"Oh! thank you."

Published in *Criterion* (St. Louis) on 13 March 1897.

So there it remained unmolested till the reviewers and others began to get in their work. Then a sudden interest in that volume awoke among people I knew, moving them to borrow; and the young folks began to pick it up and turn it over, in some instances attempting to read it. If any one of them succeeded in reading it from start to finish (which I believe is not the case) he is to be congratulated upon the achievement of having surmounted obstacles the like of which have never before confronted the seeker after entertainment.

From beginning to end there is not a gleam of humor in the book. From beginning to end there is not a line, a thought, a suggestion which could be called seductive. Its brutality is an obvious and unhappy imitation of the great French realist. The characters are so plainly constructed with the intention of illustrating the purposes of the author, that they do not for a moment convey any impression of reality. A gloom which is never lightened pervades the pages. The art is so poor that scenes intended to be impressive are at best but grotesque. The whole exposition is colorless. The hero arouses so little sympathy that at the close one does not care whether he lives or dies; he might be put upon the rack and submitted to unspeakable torture, and I am sure nobody would object; for no one minds much about the spilling of sawdust or the wrenching of rubber joints! A villainous brute of a woman commits deeds that ought by right (if the author knows his craft) to make the hair of the person who reads of them stand on end; but somehow they don't. You will just keep on munching a cream chocolate, or wondering if the postman has gone by or if there is coal on the furnace.

The book is detestably bad; it is unpardonably dull; and immoral, chiefly because it is not true.

It seems rather irrelevant and late in the day to say all this about *Jude the Obscure*. It is only sympathy for the young person which moves me to do so. I hate to know that deceptions are being practised upon him. He has been led to believe that the work is dangerous and alluring. Failing to obtain it at the libraries he is quite convinced that it is pernicious and altogether delightful, whereupon he hurries, in some instances, to the nearest book store and spends his week's allowance in procuring it. I feel very sorry to think that he should part with so many good silver quarters and receive nothing in return but disappointment and disillusion.

After all, that investigating spirit in the young person is in no sense peculiar, or is it to be wondered at or condemned. It is a characteristic shared in common with the rest of the human race, to seek to unravel

mysteries and things hidden and denied. There are the scientists, prob-
ing the heavens for its secrets, delving in the depths of the earth for
what they may discover. And what about explorers, Theosophists,
Hoodoos?

I should like to say to the young people that books which are withheld from their perusal are usually not worth reading. They are not
worth bothering about or going to any trouble or expense to obtain. If
they are written by thoughtful men, they are not addressed to the
youthful imagination and are not fashioned to be comprehended by
such. If they are written by other than thoughtful people, there is apt to
be no truth in them, and they cannot appeal to lovers of sincerity of any
age or condition.

I once knew a very young person who, while rummaging in a bureau
drawer discovered a volume secreted in its disordered profundity. The
book was obviously in hiding, and no other than she herself was the
important personage from whom it was being hidden! She at once
locked the door, abstracted the volume, and sat herself down to its
perusal. Expectation was rampant within her. She had been scenting
mysteries in the air, and the hour of illumination was at hand! The book
was something obscure, metaphysical, hysterical. It was dull reading,
but she persevered. She would greatly rather have been up in the attic
reading *Ivanhoe*. But no one had hidden *Ivanhoe* in the far depths of a
bureau drawer—*Voilà!*

On Certain Brisk, Bright Days

On certain brisk, bright days I like to walk from my home, near Thirty-fourth street, down to the shopping district. After a few such experiments I begin to fancy that I have the walking habit. Doubtless I convey the same impression to acquaintances who see me from the car window "hot-footing" it down Olive street or Washington avenue. But in my sub-consciousness, as my friend Mrs. R— would say, I know that I have not the walking habit.

Eight or nine years ago I began to write stories—short stories which appeared in the magazines, and I forthwith began to suspect I had the writing habit. The public shared this impression, and called me an author. Since then, though I have written many short stories and a novel or two, I am forced to admit that I have not the writing habit. But it is hard to make people with the questioning habit believe this.

"Now, where, when, why, what do you write?" are some of the questions that I remember. How do I write? On a lapboard with a block of paper, a stub pen and a bottle of ink bought at the corner grocery, which keeps the best in town.

Where do I write? In a Morris chair beside the window, where I can see a few trees and a patch of sky, more or less blue.

When do I write? I am greatly tempted here to use slang and reply "any old time," but that would lend a tone of levity to this bit of confidence, whose seriousness I want to keep intact if possible. So I shall say I write in the morning, when not too strongly drawn to struggle with the intricacies of a pattern, and in the afternoon, if the temptation to try a new furniture polish on an old table leg is not too powerful to be denied; sometimes at night, though as I grow older I am more and more inclined to believe that night was made for sleep.

"Why do I write?" is a question which I have often asked myself and never very satisfactorily answered. Story-writing—at least with me—is the spontaneous expression of impressions gathered goodness knows where. To seek the source, the impulse of a story is like tearing a flower to pieces for wantonness.

Published in *St. Louis Post Dispatch* on 26 November 1899.

Part 2

What do I write? Well, not everything that comes into my head, but much of what I have written lies between the covers of my books.

There are stories that seem to write themselves, and others which positively refuse to be written—which no amount of coaxing can bring to anything. I do not believe any writer has ever made a "portrait" in fiction. A trick, a mannerism, a physical trait or mental characteristic go a very short way towards portraying the complete individual in real life who suggests the individual in the writer's imagination. The "material" of a writer is to the last degree uncertain, and I fear not marketable. I have been told stories which were looked upon as veritable gold mines by the generous narrators who placed them at my disposal. I have been taken to spots supposed to be alive with local color. I have been introduced to excruciating characters with frank permission to use them as I liked, but never, in any single instance, has such material been of the slightest service. I am completely at the mercy of unconscious selection. To such an extent is this true, that what is called the polishing up process has always proved disastrous to my work, and I avoid it, preferring the integrity of crudities to artificialities.

How hard it is for one's acquaintances and friends to realize that one's books are to be taken seriously, and that they are subject to the same laws which govern the existence of others' books! I have a son who is growing wroth over the question: "Where can I find your mother's books, or latest book?"

"The very next time any one asks me that question," he exclaimed excitedly, "I am going to tell them to try the stock yards!"

I hope he won't. He might thus offend a possible buyer. Politeness, besides being a virtue, is sometimes an art. I am often met with the same question, and I always try to be polite. "My latest book? Why, you will find it, no doubt, at the bookseller's or the libraries."

"The libraries! Oh, no, they don't keep it." She hadn't thought of the bookseller's. It's real hard to think of everything! Sometimes I feel as if I should like to get a good, remunerative job to do the thinking for some people. This may sound conceited, but it isn't. If I had space (I have plenty of time; time is my own, but space belongs to the *Post-Dispatch*), I should like to demonstrate satisfactorily that it is not conceited.

I trust it will not be giving away professional secrets to say that many readers would be surprised, perhaps shocked, at the questions which some newspaper editors will put to a defenseless woman under the guise of flattery.

108

For instance: "How many children have you?" This form is subtle and greatly to be commended in dealing with women of shy and retiring propensities. A woman's reluctance to speak of her children has not yet been chronicled. I have a good many, but they'd be simply wild if I dragged them into this. I might say something of those who are at a safe distance—the idol of my soul in Kentucky; the light of my eye off in Colorado; the treasure of his mother's heart in Louisiana—but I mistrust the form of their displeasure, with poisoned candy going through the mails.

"Do you smoke cigarettes?" is a question which I consider impertinent, and I think most women will agree with me. Suppose I do smoke cigarettes? Am I going to tell it out in meeting? Suppose I don't smoke cigarettes. Am I going to admit such a reflection upon my artistic integrity, and thereby bring upon myself the contempt of the guild?

In answering questions in which an editor believes his readers to be interested, the victim cannot take herself too seriously.

Part 3

THE CRITICS

Introduction

The critical essays included here span a quarter of a century, from Per Seyersted's 1969 analysis of "The Storm" to Emily Toth's discussion of *A Vocation and a Voice*, written for this volume. Each focuses on a well-known story, a group of stories, or a volume of stories. They suggest a broad spectrum of critical approaches to Chopin's short fiction.

Anna Shannon Elfenbein's treatment of the often-discussed "Désirée's Baby" leads her to provocative questions: "Does Désirée come to believe that she is racially mixed? Does she look at Armand and see that he is racially mixed? When she looks at the quadroon child and her own child and then at Armand's dark face, does she see that Armand could be the father of both children? Does Armand suspect his racial 'taint' subconsciously? What is La Blanche's origin? Has Armand had a sexual relationship with La Blanche, and, if so, did that relationship continue after his marriage to Désirée, as might be suggested by Désirée's remark that Armand can hear their baby crying 'as far away as La Blanche's cabin' " (131).

Susan Lohafer approaches Chopin's richest short story with the sensitivity it calls for. Her reading of "Athénaïse," which she calls a nineteenth-century "classic," reveals a double pattern of changes: "the dominant linearity of Athénaïse's change, shows a progression from retreat to assertion; . . . the secondary linearity of her husband's change, shows a progression from assertion to abeyance. Taken together, they give the story a complexity and balance that most thematic readings have missed. The *Kairos* of the story, the humanly significant span of time it covers, is clearly a period of maturation. But it includes not only the woman's but the man's awakening" (132).

Peggy Skaggs writes about several *Night in Acadie* stories that "center around children." "Evidence that Chopin knew and loved children," she writes, "should be considered when analyzing Edna's ambivalent attitude toward her young sons in *The Awakening*. The children in the *Acadie* stories affect the lives of adults in varied ways. They heal, pacify, enlighten, comfort, and love. Even when they act mischievously, good often results" (27).

Mary E. Papke argues that in "The Story of an Hour" Chopin offers a reader only "one point of identification—Louise, whose powers of reflection have been repressed, suddenly shocked into being, and then brutally cut off. It is a disorienting reading experience to be cut off as well after being awakened to Louise's new self-possibilities. It is also beyond irony to be left at the conclusion with the knowledge that only Louise and the reader perceived the earlier 'death' of the true woman Mrs. Mallard; and that what murdered her was, indeed, a monstrous joy, the birth of individual self, and the erasure of that joy when her husband and, necessarily, her old self returned" (64).

Emily Toth, who in 1991 edited the first published edition of Chopin's *A Vocation and a Voice*, speculates on the reasons Chopin's publisher chose not to go ahead with the volume after the publication of *The Awakening*. For decades scholars wrote that the critical reception of the novel convinced the publisher to pull back from a commitment to publish the book of stories. In her 1990 biography, Toth suggested other possibilities. Now she reexamines the issue.

Barbara C. Ewell calls "A Pair of Silk Stockings" a "small masterpiece" and examines it alongside "Nég Créol" because both stories focus on "a portrait of the struggle for self-respect among the poor." Mrs. Sommers, she says, is "literally weakened by her devotion to others" and so "unprepared for the real battle about to engage her: not the 'breast-works of shirting and figured lawn,' but the subtler struggles with self-indulgence." Chicot, she adds, "is one of Chopin's final and most sensitive portrayals of an Afro-American" (118–22).

Per Seyersted's inclusion of "The Storm" in his *Complete Works* set the story on its way to becoming one of Kate Chopin's best-known works. Chopin, he writes, "is not consciously speaking as a woman, but as an individual. Even her previous writings had been free from misandry and from suggestions of either sex being superior to the other. In the present story, there is no trace of the covert bitterness of 'Athénaïse,' nor any complaint like Edna's that women learn so little of life. There is no antagonism or competition between Alcée and Calixta, no wilful domination in his manner or subservience in hers, even though he is higher up in society than she. In short, Mrs. Chopin appears to have achieved that thing—comparatively rare even today: to become a woman author who could write on the two sexes with a large degree of detachment and objectivity" (169).

Anna Shannon Elfenbein on "Désirée's Baby"

"Désirée's Baby" . . . is a story of peripeteia and doom. Held in a narrative balance through images of dark and light, power and powerlessness, lust and love, it moves with relentless intensity to a foregone, tragic conclusion: Désirée, the apotheosis of white wifehood and motherhood in Victorian terms, finds that the son she has borne her slaveholding husband, Armand, is a mulatto. When she beseeches Armand to explain how this can be so, he accuses her of not being white. Crushed by Armand's rejection of her, Désirée disappears with her infant into the bayou; only later does Armand discover in a letter written by his mother to his father that he himself "belongs to the race that is cursed with the brand of slavery" (1:245).

Although inadvertent miscegenation provides the plot line for "Désirée's Baby," race becomes only one more counter in the conflict that follows inevitably from the rigid categories Armand Aubigny seeks to impose on experience. Armand's power to impose a false dichotomy on all aspects of his experience is ultimately self-destructive because the world Chopin portrays admits of love that defies the rigid polarities of "black" and "white" in the case of Armand's parents' love for each other, Désirée's love for the baby, and Madame Valmondé's love for Désirée even after she perceives the color of Désirée's child. The shadowy and enigmatic presence of La Blanche on the Aubigny plantation reveals Armand's power over women but also his powerlessness to make the world conform to reductive racial categories. The irony of Armand's insistence on a dualistic view is stressed by the fact that his world is filled with mixed racial types like La Blanche and that he himself is mixed. In marrying Désirée, so visibly white, and in fathering a baby also apparently white, at least for three months, Armand may have assuaged his secret subconscious racial fears. A dark-skinned aristocrat

From Anna Shannon Elfenbein, *Women on the Color Line: Evolving Stereotypes and the Writings of George Washington Cable, Grace King, and Kate Chopin* (Charlottesville: University Press of Virginia, 1989), 126–31. Used by permission of the University Press of Virginia.

who may vaguely remember his racially mixed mother (he was eight years old when he left Paris, where his parents lived together), Armand is the only racially obsessed character in Chopin's story. Therefore, Armand's ability to define and dismiss Désirée on the basis of an arbitrary conception of racial distinctions has its penalties for him as well as for her.

The inequitable nature of these penalties, however, only becomes clear when we stop to look at the consequences of permuting the possible variations of the roles that color might play in the story. We see that if Armand is white and Désirée is white, he may hold her against her will and maintain illicit relationships with other women on the side or cast her out on any pretext and without appeal. The presumption of her infidelity would be sufficient to end the marriage, whereas the proof of his infidelity would be insufficient. If he is white and she is black, he may cast her out or relegate her to the status of La Blanche and make a house slave of their son. If Armand is black, Désirée may be vindicated by the discovery that she is not responsible for the racial characteristics of their child, but she will be forever stigmatized socially by the fact that she has been possessed by a black man and has borne his son. Désirée is clearly in a powerless position. The unresolved ambiguity about her racial identity—for we know no more about her actual origins at the end of the story than at the beginning—suggests the fact of her powerlessness: It does not really matter whether she is white or black, since her very life depends on the whims, social class, and race of her husband.

The most exquisite irony of the story, since it reflects the full extent of Désirée's powerlessness, is her name. Because she is female, Désirée's life depends upon being desired, but her life begins and ends with the antithesis of desire, abandonment. The irony of Désirée's situation is further intensified by her trust in men who betray her. When she is found by Monsieur Valmondé, who becomes her adoptive father, she awakens crying for the "Dada" (1:240) who has abandoned her. Later, she trusts in Armand to interpret reality for her when she discovers that their baby has Negroid features, and he rejects her. Thus, even when Désirée is desired, that desire is conditional. Armand's hubris, the result of male privilege buttressed by family pride and a sense of racial superiority, makes unconditional love for Désirée impossible.

In Chopin's compressed prose, the years between Désirée's discovery by Monsieur Valmondé and her marriage to Armand Aubigny flash by, but Désirée remains the same "beautiful and gentle, affectionate and

sincere" (1:240) girl that she was as a toddler. The negotiations of Valmondé and Aubigny for Désirée's marriage signal the transfer of power
from father to husband, not a rite of passage to adulthood. Thus, when
Madame Valmondé looks forward to visiting Désirée and her baby at
L'Abri, her new home, Madame thinks with amusement that "it seemed
but yesterday that Désirée was little more than a baby herself" (1:240).
When Madame Valmondé greets Désirée, she finds her lying among soft
white muslin and laces with her infant beside her, passive and inert,
changed but unchanging.

The fact that Désirée is a foundling makes possible Armand's conclusion that Désirée must be racially "tainted"; after all, *he* has a name that
is "one of the oldest and proudest in Louisiana" (1:241). Chopin's reference to the "prevailing belief . . . that [Désirée] had been purposely
left" (1:240) adds another dimension, perhaps suggesting something
about the "prevailing" attitude toward girl children. In a conventional
observation about Armand's joy at the birth of a son, Désirée herself
attributes this prejudice to Armand: "Oh, Armand is the proudest father
in the parish, I believe, chiefly because it is a boy, to bear his name;
though he says not,—that he would have loved a girl as well. But I know
it is n't true. I know he says that to please me" (1:242).

Our sense of the conventionality of Désirée's happy admission adds
to the poignance of the scene between Désirée and Madame Valmondé,
for Madame Valmondé perceives but cannot tell Désirée that her infant
is a mulatto. Finally happy because she has managed at last to completely please her husband, Désirée confides in her foster mother the
details of Armand's transformation since the baby's birth. Obviously
more important to Armand than Désirée suspects, the birth of a "white"
son has dispelled those occasional frowns that marriage to Désirée had
not fully obliterated. Désirée assures Madame Valmondé, despite
Madame's premonitions, that everything is perfect now that the baby
has come. Yet, despite Armand's joy, Désirée is desperate to please him.
Chopin suggests the difficulty of doing so and emphasizes the isolation
of Désirée in the home "which for many years had not known the gentle presence of a mistress." Such a place is no place for a woman or a
slave: "Young Aubigny's rule was a strict one, too, and under it his
negroes had forgotten how to be gay, as they had been during the old
master's easy-going and indulgent lifetime" (1:241).

This is not to say, of course, that L'Abri "shelters" no women, for
Désirée has a mulatto nurse named Zandrine for her baby, and La
Blanche lives somewhere on the plantation in a cabin with her quadroon

sons, one of whom has been given to Désirée to serve the new baby. La Blanche's palpable absence hints at the reality that will shatter Désirée's romantic illusions. Significantly, Désirée becomes conscious of La Blanche only at the moment she awakens to the truth of her own situation. Therefore, La Blanche's importance is as clear as her origins are hazy. The possibility that she may be Désirée's predecessor, sent to the slave quarters for having given birth to a mulatto son, is implied by the dark parallel Armand draws when he compares the two women. La Blanche's existence reveals the distance between Désirée's romantic illusions about marriage and her experience of a marriage that requires social hypocrisy and the innocence of its victim.

In Désirée's happy prattle to Madame Valmondé about Armand's pleasure at the birth of a son, the necessity for Désirée's self-deception about Armand's character is striking. Désirée can recognize neither the possible implications of Armand's transformation nor the fact that conditional transformations are always subject to reversal when conditions change. Accepting Armand Aubigny's "imperious and exacting nature" (1:242) as the ground of her being, Désirée must find a way to be happy, even if that way means lying to herself and attempting to justify her husband's behavior to her mother. Désirée's reason for pleasure and a temporary sense of power over her husband is his sudden kindness to his slaves. As Désirée whispers to her mother about Armand's behavior since the birth of his son, she betrays the situation: "And mamma," . . . "he has n't punished one of them—not one of them—since baby is born. Even Négrillon, who pretended to have burnt his leg that he might rest from work—he only laughed, and said Négrillon was a great scamp. Oh, mamma, I'm so happy; it frightens me" (1:242).

Désirée's sense of foreboding emphasizes her sensitivity to the powerlessness of her position. She must watch for Armand's moods to shift as they have before when he "frowned" and "she trembled, but loved him" (1:242). Recognizing Désirée's helplessness and her own, Madame Valmondé does not tell Désirée her discovery about the baby, just as she did not express her concerns about Désirée's marriage.

Because the antithetical characterizations of Désirée and Armand evoke other tragic pairings in romantic fiction, we can see that they too are trapped by sexist conventions that govern marriage as well as by racist notions that seal their fateful interaction. Bound together by all that divides them, they are victims of Armand's disastrous urges, his presumption of his right to impose his will on slaves and women. Both suffer from a fatal lack of self-knowledge. Neither can afford the luxury of seeing the world as it is. Perhaps in the uncritical adoption of the rigid roles they play, Armand and Désirée find the only secure identities available to them. These identities, Chopin implies, offer no real security at all.

Although, on reflection, we perceive the similarities between Armand and Désirée, our sympathies are engaged by Désirée. The imagery that surrounds her as she takes that last walk to the bayou is reminiscent of depictions of saints and martyrs, for Désirée is enveloped in a nimbus of light playing in golden gleams on her hair. Her tender feet and diaphanous white gown are torn by the stubble. Armand, on the other hand, is described as being possessed by "the very spirit of Satan" (1:242), and this description is reinforced by his penultimate gesture in burning all of Désirée's effects in a pyre with the help of his slave minions.

If this traditional contrast were the story's only claim on our imagination, we might resist its calculated design and dismiss it. The subtlety of the story and its extraordinary imaginative power, however, are evident. Despite the obvious patterns that set up the contrast between Désirée and Armand and prepare for the role reversal at the end, "Désirée's Baby" cannot be dismissed. Its power lies in its brevity and its lack of authorial moralizing, in its unexpected inversion of a familiar stereotype, and in the series of interlocking functional ambiguities that Chopin deploys to emphasize the meaning of Désirée's tragedy. Building to a climax from Désirée's moment of discovery to Armand's moment of discovery, these ambiguities reveal in horrifying detail the extent of Armand's power.

Désirée is, of course, the last to perceive the racial characteristics that become more pronounced as the baby's features develop. A mother's love does not depend upon race, Chopin seems to suggest, for Madame Valmondé, believing as she must that Désirée is racially mixed, tells her in a letter to come "back to your mother who loves you" (1:243) when Désirée asks for assurance that she is not contaminated by black blood. But in spite of her unwillingness to admit that she is in peril, Désirée has noticed Armand's coldness and is distraught by behavior "which she dared not ask him to explain" (1:242). Her whole world is shaken. Disorientation and inability to perceive reality replace self-assurance. Looking aimlessly from one of La Blanche's quadroon boys to her own child, Désirée sees for the first time the resemblance between the two half-naked children: " 'Ah!' it was a cry that she could not help; which she was not conscious of having uttered. The blood turned like ice in her veins, and a clammy moisture gathered upon her face" (1:242).

Does Désirée recognize a racial resemblance, a family resemblance, or both? Whatever Désirée knows or suspects, she seeks Armand for an explanation: "Look at our child. What does it mean? tell me," Désirée asks. In answering, Armand springs to the attack: " 'It means,' he answered lightly, 'that the child is not white; it means that you are not white.' " Armand's simple deduction and his laconic coldness sting Désirée: "A quick conception of all that this accusation meant for her nerved her with unwonted courage to deny it. 'It is a lie, it is not true, I am white! Look at my hair, it is brown; and my eyes are gray, Armand, you know they are gray. And my skin is fair,' seizing his wrist. 'Look at my hand; whiter than yours, Armand,' she laughed hysterically. 'As white as La Blanche's,' he returned cruelly; and went away leaving her alone with their child" (1:243).

Whatever Désirée knows, she knows that she is no longer desired. Her question, which Armand answers incorrectly, brings into focus a series of unanswerable questions that linger in the reader's mind long after the story is finished: Does Désirée know that she is adopted? What is her origin? What is her race? Does Désirée come to believe that she is racially mixed? Does she look at Armand and see that he is racially mixed? When she looks at the quadroon child and her own child and then at Armand's dark face, does she see that Armand could be the father of both children? Does Armand suspect his racial "taint" subconsciously? What is La Blanche's origin? Has Armand had a sexual relationship with La Blanche, and, if so, did that relationship continue after his marriage to Désirée, as might be suggested by Désirée's remark that Armand can hear their baby crying "as far away as La Blanche's cabin" (1:241)?

In confronting these questions, the reader must come to see the one indisputable fact—Désirée's total powerlessness—the result of the life-and-death power of the husband in her society. For whatever is actually the case about Désirée's understanding or Armand's conscious guilt, Armand has the ability to make Désirée pay for *his* transgressions, as La Blanche, we may infer, has also paid. The only recourse for Désirée is to a heavenly Father, and His good will toward women is suspect, since Madame Valmondé's prayers for Désirée and Madame Aubigny's prayers for Armand have been answered with tragedy. This final awareness leaves the reader little satisfaction other than the aesthetic satisfaction of seeing a complex view of experience validated.

Susan Lohafer on "Athénaïse"

The first word of "Athénaïse" is—"Athénaïse." Here is the first paragraph:

> Athénaïse went away in the morning to make a visit to her parents,
> ten miles back on rigolet de Bon Dieu. She did not return in the
> evening, and Cazeau, her husband, fretted not a little. He did not
> worry much about Athénaïse, who, he suspected, was resting only too
> content in the bosom of her family; his chief solicitude was manifestly
> for the pony she had ridden. He felt sure those "lazy pigs," her broth-
> ers, were capable of neglecting it seriously. This misgiving Cazeau
> communicated to his servant, old Félicité, who waited upon him at
> supper. (p. 426)

Although the wife's name is the opening word, and although the verb
sends her off on a journey, the reader is left behind with the husband.
Athénaïse "went away"—the diction is almost childlike, and certainly
the intensity is low at this point—but it takes us only four prepositional
phrases to learn what we'd know if we were living in Cazeau's world:
when ("in the morning"), why ("to make a visit"), and where ("ten
miles back on the rigolet de Bon Dieu"). The information is mostly for
our benefit, to get us very quickly over the ontological gap between our
world and the story's—but it is very circumstantial. Very inconclusive.

And now it seems that we get a series of unexpected reversals,
denials, replacements. First of all, the beginning of the second sentence
withholds the natural complement of the first sentence. The simplest
closure, our natural guess, would be: "And she returned in the evening
[to resume her life with her husband in his home on Cane River]." In
fact what we get is: "She did not return in the evening. . . ." We're left
with the direction of "away," the temporariness of "visit," and the syn-
tactic and lexical need for "return." What is preventing this closure? At
the moment, only the semantic gap between "here" and "ten miles

Reprinted by permission of Louisiana State University Press from *Coming to Terms with the
Short Story*, by Susan Lohafer. © 1983 by Louisiana State University Press.

back," between "her parents" and "her husband." How long can the separation be maintained? How great is the disequilibrium? The answer is the length and the shape of the story.

As we have in the past, let's look at the way syntax and semantics distribute intensity. I mentioned before that "went away" seems very neutral, certainly by comparison with other verbs like "ran away" or "sneaked away." And there seems to be something even more deliberately low-keyed about "fretted not a little." About his wife? Apparently not—but the stated object of his worry lies on the other side of a semicolon. Before we get there we encounter a long relative clause; within it we find the wryness of "suspected," which seems to put bitterness into "only too content," and maybe even sours the sentiment of "in the bosom of her family." Finally we do learn that his worry is for the pony his wife was riding. The family which opens its bosom to Athénaïse is "capable of seriously neglecting" the animal. It does seem strange that the words of apparently deepest and most genuine feeling are reserved for the pony, while there seems to be a grudging tone in the comments on the wife. The valences call attention to themselves, and so we register both the semantically high intensity of words like "seriously" and "chief" *and* the contextually high intensity of the flat or hackneyed diction. In the prose of this story, in its reality warp, the density and intensity are clues to what is *not* on the page.

We've seen the pony moved into the place where we'd expect Athénaïse as the object of her husband's concern. But we've also seen the Miché family moved into the role of the girl's protector. They've replaced Cazeau, and his fear that they will mistreat his pony is at least in part an expression of his own hurt feelings. The energy of his resentment comes through in his heightened concern for the pony and in his contempt for "those lazy pigs, her brothers." It's also likely that, by confiding (up to a point) in his servant, he makes her loyal presence a reproach to his wife. At any rate, there is a sense in which the story can be read only by seeing through the disguise of the text. It's not hard to do. The rules are those of the simplest psychology.

Reading further, we could say that the grammar of expectation keeps us wondering when Athénaïse will come back. Surely the absence of the wife calls loudly for her presence. Yet the story which most critics have felt to be about her frustration has up to now told us only of his. We come to believe in his love despite apparent denials: the show of not caring, maintained for pride's sake; the jangling spur which he wears indoors and which is so patent a symbol of his masculine invasion of the woman's domain; the managerial busyness of his evening work. But now look—the deepening dusk, muted sounds of crying and singing, and later the moonlight, and the "touch of the cool breath of the spring night," the "distant, tireless, plaintive notes of the accordion"—all these images crowd into the world of the story. What are they doing there?

Ostensibly, the last paragraphs of part one are about the failure of a marriage. But again, what Cazeau puts into words, even within his own thoughts, is not all that the prose has to say. It is not, as the words declare, the "unpleasant reflections" on his marriage that hold him awake, but the "touch" of the air and its sounds. "The craving of his whole body" is not, as the proposition states, "for rest and sleep"; it is for Athénaïse. We have been taught to make these substitutions by the adjustments we have had to make to enter the world of this story.

Considering the way we are drawn in, it seems to me more important to establish what we know of the story's world than to paraphrase its themes. As we have in the past, let's begin by examining what gives the story its linear dimension. Several answers are possible, but surely one of the most obvious is this: the stages of maturation from girlhood to wife-and-motherhood (defined as the awakening of the maternal and, concomitantly, the sexual instincts). I would argue that there is also a second and complementary maturation in Cazeau. Let me sketch out both sequences with some further commentary along the way. For Athénaïse,

$$X_1 = \text{a physical retreat to the rigolet de Bon Dieu.}$$

It would seem as though the wife is trying to regain the status of daughter and sister, to go back several months in time by going "ten miles back" in the bayous. What she does not like are the physical changes of marriage—the dislocation from girlhood, from a life without serious commitments. In her home the mother and younger son are weak-willed and foolish, and the father and older son, though capable of respecting the solid virtues of Cazeau, are nevertheless only renters on the land. Cazeau is an owner. Athénaïse is moving back, temporarily and geographically, to the more casual bonds of life as a Miché.

$$X_2 = \text{a psychological retreat into a sense of injury.}$$

When she has been brought back against her will, Athénaïse seeks comfort in tears and seclusion. She refuses to take Cazeau's hand offered in token of his willingness to make the best of things, and she rejects her role as mistress of the house by flinging away her bunch of keys. Finally, thinking "that Montéclin was the only friend left to her in the world," she confides her misery to him and accedes to his plan for escape.

X_3 = the physical escape to New Orleans.

Despite the provisions made by Montéclin, and despite the fact that she had been to the city in previous years, Athénaïse is for the first time on her own. True, she is not yet financially independent, but she has gallant—and quite naïve—hopes of finding a job. Her change in locale brings with it a drastic change in her manner of life, most especially freeing her from the supervision of those who have hitherto been responsible for her. On a minor scale, but on a daily basis, she is free to decide what to do.

X_4 = adoption of Gouvernail as friend, brother
surrogate, and potential lover.

This change is not really a "retreat." Athénaïse initiates the relationship with Gouvernail by asking him to address and post a letter to her brother—thus making him an innocent accomplice in her adventure. Soon she is pouring out her troubles to his surprised but sympathetic ear. He reciprocates by lending her a magazine to read, and their friendship quickly develops. It serves to introduce Athénaïse to a life of respectable but otherwise unavailable pleasures—visits to the lake, strolls through the French Quarter, little dinners in charming restaurants. It seems that the progression of events might very well lead to an X_5 which should be the acceptance of Gouvernail as a lover.

But all along there has been an undocumented series of X's, namely the physiological consequences of her marriage. These have been hinted at, but only in terms of the offensive intrusion of her husband into her life, her privacy, and, of course, her body. Suddenly the results come to the surface of the story as they come into the consciousness of the heroine:

X_5 = the discovery that she is with child by Cazeau.

Almost everyone writing about this story has quoted the passage in which this "turning point" occurs. Knowledge of her pregnancy does, of course, reverse the direction of Athénaïse's movements in the story, both the retreat from marriage and the attraction to Gouvernail. But we can see that the *peripeteia* is only an illusion created by her delayed awareness. We have seen her resent her husband's ability to carry on his work in the face of her life-shattering troubles—a telling sign that she wants him to care. We have also learned that Gouvernail, an expert on women, suspects she is really in love with her husband. And certainly, as many have noted, the lush imagery of springtime sounds and smells creates the context for a sensual awakening, for the breeding of life.

Personal and social factors have caused the readiness for adult sexuality (Eros) to be out of phase with the timing of the legal marriage (Hymen). The natural cycles of the year and of the womb are the true arbiters of maturity; when they so determine, the woman is born. In other words, the "knowledge" that Sylvie imparts does not educate the girl in any conceptual sense. It merely identifies the biological truth which must eventually dawn on her. And now we remember what everyone—except Cazeau—seems to have known from the start: "People often said that Athénaïse would know her own mind some day. . . . If she ever came to such knowledge, it would be by no intellectual research, by no subtle analyses or tracing the motives of actions to their source. It would come to her as the song to the bird, the perfume and color to the flower" (p. 433). Those who think Chopin does not understand motivation may not understand the implications of these words. Everywhere the imagery reinforces the linear process of natural organic maturation as a force stronger than logical reasoning, stronger than "motive." One "learns" the qualities of being a woman by growing into womanhood.

$$X_6 = \text{the assumption of the roles of wife and mother.}$$

As several critics have pointed out, the closure here is definitive and satisfying within the terms of the story world. Very literally, this is a homecoming story. Athénaïse returns to the husband she left, and the distant cry of the Negro baby, heard in the first section of the story, is there again at the end; it triggers the final, symbolic gesture of maternal concern.

But what of Cazeau? I mentioned earlier that he, too, experiences a growth of awareness. We might look at the stages of his maturation as a secondary but essential part of the structure. For Cazeau,

$$Y_1 = \text{denial of deepest feelings.}$$

As a temporarily deserted husband, Cazeau "fretted not a little" in that first paragraph. We've seen that he does not admit his real feelings but hides them behind concern—quite genuine in itself—for the pony. He maintains an air of business as usual. It is this very capacity for self-discipline which aggravates Athénaïse's resentment. But we see beyond it to the feeling it guards, to the yearning which Cazeau does not even admit to himself.

Y_2 = forces Athénaïse to return to his home.

Cazeau finds Athénaïse's continued absence an annoyance. Retrieving her will be an inconvenience in his busy workday, but he sees it as "the task of bringing his wife back to a sense of her duty." When he confronts her in her parents' home and receives her look of reproach, he is "maddened and wounded. . . . But whatever he might feel, Cazeau [knows] only one way to act toward a woman" (p. 431). That "way" is with gentleness and courtesy but with a firmness that allows for no question of his right to give orders. Cazeau's range of responsiveness here is clearly limited. He knows "only one way to act" toward all those in the category of "women." This class noun identifies a category that is not only biologically but socially conditioned for obedience. Generalizations about women are so engrained that they preempt any special consideration of the narrower categories, "inexperienced girls" and "Athénaïse." Cazeau has no equipment for dealing with the confused emotions of this particular woman. Neither can he allow his own particular feelings to interfere with what he conceives to be his duty as the man in charge—of his workers, his lands, his livestock, his wife.

Y_3 = gives up "story-book" notions of happiness.

Chopin's fairness, her balanced view of the battle of the sexes, is evident in Cazeau's own confessed illusions. He admits, with dignified candor, that "I expected—I was even that big a fool—I believed that yo' coming yere to me would be like the sun shining out of the clouds, an' that our days would be like w'at the story-books promise after the wedding. I was mistaken" (p. 435). From a less honorable man, these words would seem like recrimination. From someone whose dignity was only swagger, they might be simply ridiculous. But from Cazeau, the admission is both manly and pertinent. Men as well as women are vulnerable to romantic yearnings that have nothing to do with mundane existence or—more importantly—with genuine passion. But we see here that

Cazeau can adapt to new perceptions, can correct his presumptions. He, in his own way, can change.

Y_4 = experiences a "humiliating sensation of baseness" when passing the old oak tree.

Cazeau, too, has his burgeoning of consciousness. And, like the awakening of Athénaïse, it is triggered by a heightening of the senses rather than by a sharpening of the mind. Crossing "the old fallow meadow that was level and hard," *i.e.*, yielding no crop, Cazeau sees the tree "that had been a landmark for ages—or was it the odor of elderberry stealing up from the gully to the south? or what was it that brought vividly back to Cazeau, by some association of ideas, a scene of many years ago?" (p. 433). This may be Lockean psychology, the progress from sensation to idea, but here the "idea" remains an image, or rather a series of images which add up to a "whole impression." That impression is "hideous," but the reason for its ugliness is never specified, never rationally perceived. Later, Cazeau refrains from pursuing Athénaïse to New Orleans. Consciously he sees the matter as an issue of pride: "For no woman on earth would he again undergo the humiliating sensation of baseness that had overtaken him in passing the old oak-tree in the fallow meadow" (p. 438). But Chopin has again, as in the opening paragraph, made the prose cut two ways. That class noun "woman" has been intensified to "no woman on earth." He is now judging by life on earth, not in "storybooks." The verbs, too, are telling. Pages ago, when first passing the oak tree, Cazeau "spurred his horse to a swift gallop[, o]vertaking his wife." Now we learn that he is the one who was "overtaken." He is now also the subject of "undergo," a verb that is grammatically transitive but semantically passive. Did we think it was only Athénaïse who is undergoing duress? Cazeau, too, has been acted upon by something beyond his control.

Prompted by his new feeling, Cazeau writes Athénaïse the letter "in which he disclaimed any further intention of forcing his commands upon her." It may seem a rather stiff communication, but its tone and premises are different from those of his previous dealings with Athénaïse. The letter is addressed from one person to another, rather than from a Husband to a Wife. Cazeau is recognizing the woman he loves as someone with a will of her own, with the power to make a choice, and with the right to be a voluntary and reciprocal partner in the union of marriage. It is a letter he could not have written prior to Y_4, and it brings closure to his part of the story.

The pattern of X's, the dominant linearity of Athénaïse's change, shows a progression from retreat to assertion; the pattern of Y's, the secondary linearity of her husband's change, shows a progression from assertion to abeyance. Taken together, they give the story a complexity and balance that most thematic readings have missed. The *Kairos* of the story, the humanly significant span of time it covers, is clearly a period of maturation. But it includes not only the woman's but the man's awakening.

Viewed holistically, as a spatial design, the story is a pair of converging "biorhythms"—as they'd be called today. Gouvernail, remember, introduces the idea that marriage, as an institution, is irrelevant. What properly arranges sexual union is the mutual desire of the people involved, whether married or not. It may have been a liberal view in the 1890s; it may have been "daring" as an opinion, but as a description of the forces at work in the world, it seems only a faithful account. Since the fifties, critics have made this argument their theme. Although there has been praise for the control of imagery, the psychological realism, and the dramatic finesse of the story, that admiration fails to do justice to Chopin's appreciation of short story aesthetics. Many of her tales *are* no more than sketches or vignettes, but in "Athénaïse" she exploits the dual dimensions of linearity and spatiality, the unified *Kairos*, the emblematic sentences, and the powerful closure which help make the peculiar "resistance"—and thus the rhythm—of the short story.

Peggy Skaggs on Stories about Children

In her second volume of stories, *A Night in Acadie*, Chopin shifts emphases and concentrates particularly on love—all kinds of love: filial, fraternal, paternal, maternal, marital, sexual—although she continues to examine the various other facets of human identity as well.

Nine of the twenty-one stories center around children. Orrick Johns in a 1911 review of Chopin's *Bayou Folk* and *A Night in Acadie* says, "no such knowledge of children and no such love of them is to be found in other books."[1] This evidence that Chopin knew and loved children should be considered when analyzing Edna's ambivalent attitude toward her young sons in *The Awakening*. The children in the *Acadie* stories affect the lives of adults in varied ways. They heal, pacify, enlighten, comfort, and love. Even when they act mischievously, good often results.

In "After the Winter," for example, the interference of children brings M'sieur Michel, the protagonist, back into contact with humanity after twenty-five years of alienation. "Ripe Figs" reveals beautifully the differing perspectives on time of the child and the adult, expressing in one short page virtually the essence of the generation gap. And "A Matter of Prejudice" tells of a proud Creole woman who for ten years had refused to visit her son Henri because he is married to an "American" woman. Finally, a child's love heals this breach between the generations.

"Mamouche" carries the name of one of its central characters, a mischievous waif who turns up one rainy night at Doctor John-Luis's door and eventually brings to that bachelor physician the fulfillment he had not even known he lacked. Mamouche also figures in bringing fulfillment to two adults in "The Lilies" when he lets down the fences that separate the Widow Angèle's calf from Mr. Billy's crops. The crops suffer, but the story ends with a hint that marriage between the impoverished Widow and the wealthy but lonely Mr. Billy may follow.

"Odalie Misses Mass" tells of a little girl who stops by to "show herself" dressed up for mass on Assumption day to Aunt Pinky, her "old

Reprinted by permission of Twayne Publishers, an imprint of Simon & Schuster Macmillan, from *Kate Chopin*, by Peggy Skaggs. © 1985 by G. K. Hall & Co.
1. Orrick Johns, "The 'Cadians," *St. Louis Mirror* (10 July 1911), 5–6.

friend and protegée" (406). Finding that the ill, old black woman has been left alone while everyone else has gone to church, Odalie stays with her. After mass Odalie's mother finds both the child and the old woman asleep; but Aunt Pinky never awakens. Odalie's childish conceit, her obvious delight in displaying her new outfit, and the love that makes her miss the big occasion after all rather than leave Aunt Pinky alone—these qualities illustrate what Johns means in saying that Chopin knew and loved children.

Two stories develop the idea that a woman needs to feel maternal love, even if she has never borne a child. In "Polydore" Mamzelle Adelaide—a kind, naive, middle-aged spinster—tries faithfully to fulfill her promise made years before to Polydore's dying mother to look after the boy. Now a stupid, lazy lad of fourteen, Polydore pretends one day to be ill, thus causing Mamzelle to go out into the heat and consequently to develop a severe fever. Polydore feels dreadfully guilty. At last he confesses to Mamzelle "in a way that bared his heart to her for the first time. . . . she felt as if a kind of miracle had happened. . . . She knew that a bond of love had been forged. . . . she drew him close to her and kissed him as mothers kiss" (417). Thus through maternal love Mamzelle's good but heretofore emotionally impoverished life gains warmth and beauty.

"Regret" develops more fully this theme that to experience life richly a woman needs a child or children to love and care for. Although in the beginning Mamzelle Aurélie, the protagonist, feels perfectly satisfied, circumstances force her to recognize that her life lacks something.

Mamzelle, one of Chopin's most memorable women, "possessed a good strong figure, ruddy cheeks, . . . and a determined eye. She wore a man's hat . . . and an old blue army overcoat . . . and sometimes top-boots." Far from regretting her spinster status, "Mamzelle Aurélie had never thought of marrying. . . . and at the age of fifty she had not yet lived to regret it." Neither does she think of herself as lonely, although "she was quite alone in the world, except for her dog Ponto, and the negroes . . . and the fowls, a few cows, a couple of mules, her gun . . . and her religion" (375). But when her neighbor Odile must go away on an emergency, Mamzelle offers to care for Odile's children.

Mamzelle soon discovers that "children are not little pigs; they require . . . attentions which were wholly unexpected by Mamzelle Aurélie, and which she was ill prepared to give." In time she learns that "Marcélette always wept when spoken to in a loud and commanding tone" (376), that Ti Nomme picks all the choicest flowers in the garden and cannot sleep without being told at least one story, that Elodie must be rocked and sung to sleep—in short that each child is an individual and that each must have all the privileges and attention that individuality involves. In fact, Mamzelle confides to her cook: "I tell you . . . I'd rather manage a dozen plantation' than fo' chil'ren. It's terrassent! Bonté! Don't talk to me about chil'ren" (377).

The spinster quickly adjusts, however. She learns to accept Ti Nomme's "moist kisses—the expressions of an affectionate and exuberant nature." In a few days she becomes accustomed "to the laughing, the crying, the chattering." And by the end of two weeks, "she could sleep comfortably with little Elodie's hot plump body pressed close against her" (377).

But then Odile reclaims her brood. Mamzelle watches them leave: "The excitement was all over. . . . How still it was when they were gone!" She goes back into the house, now empty as never before: "The evening shadows were creeping and deepening around her solitary figure. She let her head fall down upon her bended arm, and began to cry. . . . She cried like a man, with sobs that seemed to tear her very soul" (378). Mamzelle again lacks that important part of a woman's life, the maternal relationship; but worse, perhaps, she can never again perceive herself as the strong, self-sufficient, satisfied planter.

Mary E. Papke on "The Story of an Hour"

"The Story of an Hour," . . . details a very ordinary reality and conscientiously analyzes that moment in a woman's life when the boundaries of the accepted everyday world are suddenly shattered and the process of self-consciousness begins. Louise Mallard, dutiful wife and true woman, is gently told that her husband has been killed in a train accident. Her response is atypical, however, and that is the subject of the story: what Louise thinks and feels as she finds herself thrust into solitude and self-contemplation for the first time.

Louise appears in the opening as the frail, genteel, devoted wife of a prosperous businessman; she is at first only named as such: Mrs. Mallard. However, her first response to the tragedy indicates a second Louise nestling within that social shell: "she did not hear the story as many women have heard the same, with a paralyzed inability to accept its significance. She wept at once, with sudden, wild abandonment, in her sister's arms" (352). Chopin thus implies that perhaps some part of Louise readily accepts the news. She also intimates that since Louise unconsciously chooses to enfold herself in a female embrace and not in the arms of the male friend who tells her of Mallard's death, Louise has already turned to a female world, one in which she is central. It is in the mid-section of the story, set in Louise's room, that Louise and Chopin's reader explore and come to understand reaction and potential action, social self—Mrs. Mallard—and private, female self—Louise.

Louise sits before an open window at first thinking nothing but merely letting impressions of the outer and inner worlds wash over her. She is physically and spiritually depleted but is still sensuously receptive. She sees the "new spring life" (352) in budding trees, smells rain, hears human and animal songs as well as a man "crying his wares" (352). She is like both a tired child dreaming a sad dream (353) and a

Mary E. Papke, *Verging on the Abyss: The Social Fiction of Kate Chopin and Edith Wharton* (Westport, CT: Greenwood Press, 1990), 62–64. © 1990 by Mary E. Papke. Reprinted with permission of Greenwood Publishing Group, Inc. All rights reserved.

young woman self-restrained but with hidden strengths. She is yet Mrs. Mallard.

As she sits in "a suspension of intelligent thought" (353), she feels something unnameable coming to her through her senses. It is frightening because it is not of her true womanhood world; it reaches to her from the larger world outside and would "possess her" (353). The unnameable is, of course, her self-consciousness that is embraced once she names her experience as emancipation and not destitution: "She said it over and over under her breath: 'free, free, free!' . . . Her pulses beat fast, and the coursing blood warmed and relaxed every inch of her body" (353). It is at this point that she begins to think, the point at which she is reborn through and in her body, an experience analogous to that of Edna Pontellier in *The Awakening*.

Louise then immediately recognizes her two selves and comprehends how each will co-exist, the old finally giving way to the one new self. Mrs. Mallard will grieve for the husband who had loved her, but Louise will eventually revel in the "monstrous joy" (353) of self-fulfillment, beyond ideological strictures and the repressive effects of love:

> she would live for herself. There would be no powerful will bending hers in that blind persistence with which men and women believe they have a right to impose a private will upon a fellow-creature. A kind intention or a cruel intention made the act seem no less a crime as she looked upon it in that brief moment of illumination.
>
> And yet she had loved him—sometimes. Often she had not. What did it matter! What could love, the unsolved mystery, count for in face of this possession of self-assertion which she suddenly recognized as the strongest impulse of her being! (353)

It is only after Louise embraces this new consciousness, her sense of personal and spiritual freedom in a new world, that she is named as female self by her sister. This is no doubt ironic since her sister only unconsciously recognizes her; she can have little idea of the revolution that has taken place in Louise's own room. Yet Chopin does not allow simple utopian endings, and Louise's sister's intrusion into Louise's world also prefigures the abrupt end to her "drinking in a very elixir of life through that open window" (354).

Louise leaves her room and descends again into her past world. Though she carries herself "like a goddess of Victory" (354) and has transcended the boundaries of her past self, she is not armed for the lethal intrusion of the past world through her front door. Brently Mallard unlocks his door and enters unharmed. His return from the dead kills Louise, and Chopin's conclusion is the critical and caustic remark that all believed "she had died of heart disease—of joy that kills" (354).

It is easy for the reader to be overwhelmed by the pathos of the story, a natural response since the reader comes to consciousness of the text just as Louise awakens to self-consciousness. Chopin offers the reader only that one point of identification—Louise, whose powers of reflection have been repressed, suddenly shocked into being, and then brutally cut off. It is a disorienting reading experience to be cut off as well after being awakened to Louise's new self-possibilities. It is also beyond irony to be left at the conclusion with the knowledge that only Louise and the reader perceived the earlier "death" of the true woman Mrs. Mallard; and that what murdered her was, indeed, a monstrous joy, the birth of individual self, and the erasure of that joy when her husband and, necessarily, her old self returned. Far from being a melodramatic ending, the conclusion both informs and warns: should a woman see the real world and her individual self within it only to be denied the right to live out that vision, then in her way lies non-sense, self-division, and dissolution. Chopin's analysis of womanhood ideology and quest for self here takes on a darker hue. Her earlier stories examined the destruction of women who lived within traditional society; this piece offers no escape for those who live outside that world but who do so only in a private world in themselves. Either way, Chopin seems to be saying, there lies self-oblivion if only the individual changes and not the world.

Emily Toth on *A Vocation and a Voice*

A Vocation and a Voice: Why Was It Killed?

The usual story goes like this: Kate Chopin was a much-acclaimed, much-loved author of charming Louisiana local color stories, especially those in *Bayou Folk* (1894). But then she published *The Awakening*, a novel that was considered poisonously sensual for 1899, and it was brutally condemned by virtually every influential reviewer. Later generations even believed (incorrectly) that it had been banned (Toth, 422–425).

In any case, not long after unleashing *The Awakening*, Chopin's publisher, Herbert S. Stone of Chicago, cancelled the contract for her next short story collection, *A Vocation and a Voice*. Why did he do so?

As Chopin's rediscoverer Per Seyersted put it in 1969: "Herbert S. Stone in February, 1900, returned the collection 'A Vocation and a Voice,' giving no reason. Not knowing that Stone had decided to reduce the number of titles to be published by his company, nor that he had been unafraid of censorship when he brought out, for example, Garland's *Rose of Dutcher's Coolly*, Kate Chopin may have thought that the rejection meant that she had become a literary outcast" (Seyersted, 182; Kramer, 298).

I echoed Seyersted in my 1990 Chopin biography, in which I wrote: "In February 1900, Kate also received some crushing news: Herbert S. Stone & Company decided not to publish her third short-story collection, *A Vocation and a Voice*. The firm was cutting back on its list, and not necessarily making a judgment on Kate Chopin's writing—but she may not have known that.

"She did not even try to find another publisher for the collection" (Toth, 373; Kramer, 298).

But now I wonder about the usual story. Perhaps Seyersted and I were too quick to exonerate Herbert S. Stone. Can we be sure that his decision was commercial, and not moral?

Kate Chopin did save some letters, most of which were eventually deposited in the Missouri Historical Society library in St. Louis. Most are fan letters cheering *The Awakening*, from St. Louis friends, and there is not a negative letter among them—which suggests that Chopin (or the descendants who kept her papers) preferred keeping optimistic materials and destroying sad or troublesome ones (Toth, chapters 22–23).

That makes it all the more ominous that Herbert S. Stone's letter cancelling *A Vocation and a Voice* seems not to be available anywhere. All we have is Chopin's notation in her manuscript account book: "R   Feb. 1900" (R was her usual symbol for "returned": Toth, Seyersted, Bonnell).

Chopin's saved letters are mostly personal rather than business ones, but Stone's business papers were saved and collected (Newberry Library, Chicago). Yet there are no letters from Herbert Stone to or about Kate Chopin. Nor are there Chopin letters to or from Lucy Monroe, Stone's reader and publishing adviser, who seems to have been responsible for the firm's buying and promoting *The Awakening*: Monroe even wrote the first notice of the novel, in *Book News* (Toth, 328–329). Possibly Lucy Monroe had left Stone & Co. by the time *A Vocation and a Voice* was cancelled.

Or maybe Daniel Rankin, Chopin's earliest biographer, was most accurate in his assessment: "Perhaps the bitter reception given *The Awakening* . . . intimidated the publishers" (195).

In recent decades, modern critical theorists have directed us to look for absences and silences and to deconstruct them—but there is no way to tell what the lack of a Stone letter means. Possibly he wrote Chopin that the firm was cutting back on its list, as Seyersted believed. But it is also possible that Stone wrote something like this to Kate Chopin (I am making this up): "The scandalous and negative response toward *The Awakening* makes publication of your next book a troubling and uncertain proposition. We are, after all, a firm dedicated to making a profit, and you are, we are sorry to say, too unpredictable and too risky an author. Nevertheless, we wish you luck in your future endeavors . . ."

Such a letter from Stone is not impossible, for *The Awakening* was not a commercial success. Chopin's royalties as of December 1899, ten months after publication, added up to $102, a larger single sum than any of her other books earned (Toth, Seyersted, Bonnell). But earlier, Chopin had been paid as much as $50 for a single short story in *Youth's Companion*—and the power of the children's market may be another reason for the killing of *A Vocation and a Voice.*

In the 1890s, the demarcation between children and adult audiences was not so firm as it is today: virtually all magazines were intended to be suitable for home and family, and were edited with "the Young Person" in mind. Truly "adult" literature was very rare—and often frowned upon—in the United States.

In *Bayou Folk,* Chopin's most favored collection, as many as half of the book's twenty-three stories could be classified as children's tales (Koloski). A typical *Bayou Folk* story takes place in rural Louisiana, with a light, bright atmosphere, quaint French touches, and few villains or signs of true evil. In most cases, the stories end happily, sometimes with romantic self-sacrifices.

But in Chopin's second collection, *A Night in Acadie* (1897), she was writing more for adults—which may also be why she published with a regional house, Chicago-based Way & Williams, rather than with Houghton, Mifflin of Boston, *Bayou Folk*'s publisher. A typical story from *A Night in Acadie* is set in Louisiana, but only about a third of the collection's twenty-one stories might be considered especially appropriate for young readers. Some of the less-suitable stories have moral ambiguities about sex ("A Respectable Woman") or death ("At Chênière Caminada," "A Sentimental Soul"). Some, such as "Ripe Figs," are sketches rather than stories with plots and characters.

With the twenty-two stories in *A Vocation and a Voice,* however, only "An Easter Day Conversion (A Morning Walk)" completely follows the pattern of children's stories. It is a holiday narrative of sweetness and redemption, with flowers and the flavor of church. But the rest of the *Vocation and a Voice* stories are adult, often sensual, and opposed to the values late Victorian American society preferred to impress upon youth.

Characters in *A Vocation and a Voice*'s stories flout convention by—among other sins—reading private mail ("Elizabeth Stock's One Story"), deceiving well-meaning nuns ("Lilacs"), smoking illicit hallucinogenic cigarettes ("An Egyptian Cigarette"), rejoicing at a husband's death ("Story of an Hour"), and condoning murder ("The Godmother"). Sexual passion appears without marriage in, among others, "Her Letters," "Two Portraits (The Nun and the Wanton)," and

"Juanita." In the title story, the central character is a boy torn between the values of the church and the pull of the flesh. In the end—very unchildlike—he chooses flesh.

A Vocation and a Voice was, of course, cancelled—smothered—before it could shock potential readers. Due to appear in 1901, it was not published as a separate collection until 90 years later, when I edited it as a Penguin Classic (Chopin). Nowadays, stories of infidelity, drugs, deceit, and murder are no longer shocking—and Herbert S. Stone's killing the collection for those reasons (if he did) seems quaint to current readers.

Yet my undergraduate students at Louisiana State University in the 1990s have admired and enjoyed *Bayou Folk*—and intensely disliked *A Vocation and a Voice*.

My students like *Bayou Folk* for many of the same reasons its original readers enjoyed it in the 1890s: the humor, the Louisiana local atmosphere, the quaint names, the small and courageous deeds, and the romances of unknown, passionate, rural people. My students from Acadian (Cajun) backgrounds especially see their grandparents in some of the tales, and they like the stories in which good people win out.

But the *Vocation and a Voice* stories strike my students as weird, strange, too similar, and frustratingly vague. The students cannot identify with the characters, who are often nameless—among them the girl in "The White Eagle," the boy in the title story, and the narrators in "An Egyptian Cigarette," "An Idle Fellow," and "The Night Came Slowly." The *Voice* stories often end in disillusionment, death, or both; often they describe obsessions, blindness, or urban blight. Or the endings are not only unexpected but distinctly peculiar, as in "The Blind Man" or "The Falling in Love of Fedora"—a story rejected in its day for not having enough plot (Toth, 296).

Also, the romances in *A Vocation and a Voice* almost invariably go awry: there is no happily ever after. Distance, disabilities, and aging all separate once-passionate lovers; young women become bored or appalled by their suitors. In at least seven stories, romances falter just because the timing is wrong ("Suzette," "The Kiss," "A Mental Suggestion," "Two Summers and Two Souls," "The Unexpected," "The Recovery," and "Ti Démon").

It is often said that, with *The Awakening*, Kate Chopin was ahead of her time: that novel is now regarded, without question, as a masterpiece. We might say that readers now know how to read, and appreciate, the story of a woman's refusal to stay in the nest, and her insistence on following her own quest. Indeed, many of the novels of the feminist 1970s follow a similar pattern as *The Awakening*. In such books as Erica Jong's *Fear of Flying*, Alix Kates Shulman's *Memoirs of an Ex-Prom Queen*, Marge Piercy's *Small Changes*, and Sue Kaufman's *Diary of a Mad Housewife*, a woman awakens from a conventional life to spread her wings and search for something new.

Yet audiences still do not, apparently, know how to read/appreciate the stories in *A Vocation and a Voice*. "The Story of an Hour," a very short tale with a surprise ending that is unsurpassed for teaching, is a perennial favorite—but most of the other *Voice* stories are too mysterious, melancholy, or sophisticated even for today's readers. Modern readers, like their predecessors, prefer stories to be neatly constructed, with beginning, middle, and end, and with a conclusion that is satisfying, complete, and upbeat.

Kate Chopin in her latter years refused to deliver such a story.

It may be that Herbert S. Stone, an avant-garde publisher who nevertheless had to keep his enterprise afloat, recognized in 1900 that *A Vocation and a Voice* would be too hard a "sell." By then other editors, too, were shying away from Kate Chopin. Although most of the *Voice* stories first appeared in *Vogue*, a new magazine edited by the eccentric Josephine Redding, few other periodicals were accepting Chopin's writings after 1900. Most tellingly: during the year of *The Awakening*, three of Chopin's children's stories were accepted by *Youth's Companion* and duly paid for—but they were never published (Toth, 373). No reason is given for that, either.

It may be coincidence that Chopin was losing her magazine and book audiences at once—but it is equally likely that she ran afoul of both for the same reasons: at age fifty in 1900, she refused to compromise her vision. It may also be that although Stone supported Hamlin Garland's somewhat earthy *Rose of Dutcher's Coolly*, he could not continue publishing a woman author who wrote so openly about sex as Kate Chopin does in, for instance, "A Vocation and a Voice" and "Two Portraits (The Nun and the Wanton)." Garland was never so explicit.

But unless other papers come to light, we can never truly know why *A Vocation and a Voice* was cancelled by Herbert S. Stone's publishing company. It may be that Stone underestimated his audience's ability to grasp subtleties and appreciate ironies—but today's readers, as my students show, have many of the same difficulties.

Stone may, in fact, have been making both a commercial and a moral decision: in his view, audiences were simply not ready for *A Vocation and a Voice.*
In that, he was almost certainly right.

Works Cited

Chopin, Kate. *A Vocation and a Voice: Stories.* Edited and with an introduction by Emily Toth. New York: Viking Penguin, 1991.

Koloski, Bernard. Personal conversation, June 1995.

Kramer, Sidney. *History of Stone & Kimball and Herbert S. Stone & Co.* Chicago: University of Chicago, 1940.

Rankin, Daniel. *Kate Chopin and Her Creole Stories.* Philadelphia: University of Pennsylvania, 1932.

Seyersted, Per. *Kate Chopin: A Critical Biography.* Baton Rouge: Louisiana State University and Oslo: Universitetsforlaget, 1969.

Toth, Emily. *Kate Chopin: A Life of the Author of "The Awakening."* New York: Morrow, 1990; Austin: University of Texas, 1993.

Toth, Emily, Per Seyersted, and Marilyn Bonnell. *Kate Chopin's Private Papers.* Bloomington: Indiana University Press, forthcoming.

Barbara C. Ewell on
"A Pair of Silk Stockings"
and "Nég Créol"

Chopin wrote two excellent stories, both featuring the urban poor. Even better than "Miss McEnders," these tales combine social criticism with acute portraiture. "A Pair of Silk Stockings" (April 1896), a small masterpiece, wastes no time on exposition:

> Little Mrs. Sommers one day found herself the unexpected possessor of fifteen dollars. It seemed to her a very large amount of money, and the way in which it stuffed and bulged her worn old *porte-monnaie* gave her a feeling of importance such as she had not enjoyed for years.

The power of money to enhance self-esteem and confidence is the core of this poignant tale. Mrs. Sommers is a "little" person, presumably a widow, with at least four children, whose poverty, evidently a result of her marriage, has considerably reduced her stature in the community. But, unlike other more romantic widows, Mrs. Sommers has "no second of time to devote to the past." The grinding present absorbs all her energies and the future is too grim to contemplate.

Evidently she has accepted her "littleness," though her intrepid spirit is manifest at bargain counter mélées and in her rapturous calculations about buying clothes and shoes for her brood. This undaunted enthusiasm does, however, take its toll. Chopin mirrors her harried state in the broken syntax that describes her self-forgetfulness on her shopping trip:

> But that day she was a little faint and tired. She had swallowed a light luncheon—no! when she came to think of it, between getting the children fed and the place righted, and preparing herself for the shopping bout, she had actually forgotten to eat any luncheon at all!

Excerpts from *Kate Chopin*, by Barbara C. Ewell. ©1986 by the Ungar Publishing Company. Reprinted by permission.

Literally weakened by her devotion to others, Mrs. Sommers is unprepared for the real battle about to engage her: not the "breast-works of shirting and figured lawn," but the subtler struggles with self-indulgence. Her first response to the shopgirl's innocent query about buying stockings is automatically selfless. But the garments then become "serpent-like," glistening and gliding through her hands until the two "hectic blotches" on her cheeks announce her capitulation. The sensuous satisfaction of the silk as she dons her purchase stills any further rational activity. Her luxurious, youthful past and the self it defined, which she has so long resisted, finally erupts. In language that directly anticipates Edna Pontellier, Mrs. Sommers relinquishes the strenuous exercise of self-discipline and "abandon[s] herself to some mechanical impulse that directed her actions and freed her of responsibility."

The extent of Mrs. Sommers's self-neglect is evident in her amazement, as she buys new shoes, that those pretty feet and ankles "belonged to her and were a part of herself." As she succumbs to each successive temptation, her confidence expands. Her new accessories give "her a feeling of assurance, a sense of belonging to the well-dressed multitude." Her final indulgence is her most frivolous, a matinée. Attended by gaudily dressed women killing time, it aptly concludes her own venture into a world of make-believe. For despite her increased ease, Mrs. Sommers has only entered this world temporarily. Her presence in this essentially materialistic society is as gratuitous and evanescent as the matinée or her fifteen dollars. The dream ends, as it must for so many of Chopin's characters—Mrs. Mallard, Adrienne, Mlle. Aurélie, Jane. Mrs. Sommers becomes "little" once more.

In a bold technical move, Chopin shifts the perspective in the last paragraph to that of a man "with keen eyes." An interested but impersonal observer, like ourselves, he cannot penetrate "the study of her small, pale face." And any confidence in our own assessment is deliberately undermined by the last sentence:

> In truth, he saw nothing—unless he were wizard enough to detect a poignant wish, a powerful longing that the cable car would never stop anywhere, but go on and on with her forever.

That Mrs. Sommers is filled with regret is clear. But regret for what? for the self-indulgence of a day with the money of a windfall? for the dissipation of an illusion of well-being? for the impossibility of freedom? for the life she has chosen? for the hungry, clamoring children who await her? Chopin lets us guess. The changes in Mrs. Sommers possess an impenetrable interiority. But there is a profound poignance in her "powerful longing" and in the poverty that created it, burdening with guilt even so small a self-indulgence.

Chopin's consciousness of poverty's effects on selfhood is equally apparent in "Nég Créol" (April 1896), which features the eccentric Chicot, clinging to the fringes of society, grasping at both survival and human dignity. As for Tante Cat'rinette, Chicot's idiosyncrasies and illusions raise him above the stereotype of the ex-slave; Chicot is one of Chopin's final and most sensitive portrayals of an Afro-American. Like "little Mrs. Sommers," Chicot is insignificant in his urban world. Even in the unselective society of the French Market, he is "so black, lean, lame, and shriveled" that "one felt privileged to call him almost anything." Chicot, however, transforms his marginality into a virtue. His wildly comic religious beliefs and his inflation of the magnificent Boisduré family (both ironic consequences of his slavery) are essential to Chicot's self-respect. And even though the last remnant of the Boisdurés is, in fact, the impoverished Mlle. Aglaé (as unable to support herself as to aggrandize her servants by their association), Chicot's devotion gives his life purpose and value.

Mademoiselle's own illusions echo these fragile claims to a fragile dignity. Like Chicot, she entrenches herself in eccentricities and intolerance to affirm her selfhood. She deliberately irritates him, challenging his odd beliefs with her own showy but more conventional devotions. Mademoiselle prefers to believe that she does not need a poor black man's charity, though, of course, she does; and she needs not only the spoils of his begging and pitiful earnings, but also his attentions to her endless complaints. Chicot bears them readily, since for him they voice a just protest against her disgraceful poverty and his own humiliation.

The balance of support between these two, however, only mirrors the larger network of charity that dignifies the lives of the poor. Not only does Chicot exist on the lagniappe of the French Market vendors, but when Mademoiselle dies, the kindness of her eccentric neighbors is manifest: "Purgatory Mary" with her Lourdes water and borrowed candlesticks, the generous Irish woman Brigitte, and even the curious but respectful "street Arabs" who attend the wake. Even Chicot's refusal to pray to the negligent "Michié bon Dieu," despite the pain of Mademoiselle's loss, marks an uncompromising devotion to their failing dignity. Similarly, when the fishmonger's Italian wife remarks that one of his famous Boisdurés has died—"po', same-a like church rat"—Chicot emphatically denies any connections with *his* Boisdurés and even declines to watch the small funeral procession wend past the Market. His apparent betrayal is, of course, intense fidelity, not only to Mademoiselle, but also to his own dignity as the former servant of the unexceptionally magnificent Boisdurés.

This portrait of the struggle for self-respect among the poor recalls an earlier treatment of the same theme, "A Gentleman of Bayou Têche." But the shift from the lush Têche countryside to the urban bustle of New Orleans marks the distance between *A Night in Acadie* (of which "Nég Créol" was the latest story included) and *Bayou Folk*. In the earlier story, Evariste needs no illusions to confirm his gentlemanhood; he earns the title by his deed; only outsiders like Mr. Sublet must learn to penetrate the facade of his poverty, to see more than "local color." But for Chicot, illusions are the only substance, since no amount of generosity or service or self-sacrifice could in contemporary Euro-American eyes elevate a poor Afro-American to the dignity of gentleman. Chicot's eccentricities, even his poverty, have become his essence. His life does not reflect, but *is* local color. Evariste's quaint surfaces, when one sees them without prejudice, reveal the hidden realities of his human dignity. For Chicot those eccentric appearances are intrinsic to his selfhood. Rather than penetrate his surfaces, one must comprehend the peculiar reality of Chicot's perceptions: see how he sees, and recognize the value that vision comprehends. As for later modernists like James or Faulkner, perspective itself proves as powerful an element of fiction as any precise delineation of its contents.

Per Seyersted on "The Storm"

Sex is never comic in Kate Chopin's writings. In "The Storm" it is so elated and "happy," so full of joy that we are reminded of the *Song of Solomon*, which it parallels also in its use of the lily and the pomegranate. The story leaves aside all suspense of plot; while Clarisse in "At the 'Cadian Ball" plays with Alcée before she catches him, Calixta shows here no "guile or trickery." The author concentrates instead on the delights of *sexe pur.* There is nothing to hide in this naked pleasure, she seems to say as she discards the bird and the idealized representation of Maupassant's *conte.* Surpassing that "courage . . . of our perceptions" which Henry James had observed in the Frenchman, Mrs. Chopin turned to the matter at hand without circumlocutions. Particularly the love-making scene is an example of her courage to treat the forbidden and of her stylistic daring in describing it with the unreserved directness and supreme authenticity of truth.[1]

Sex in this story is a force as strong, inevitable, and natural as the Louisiana storm which ignites it. Given the opportunity, imperative Eros will, for better or for worse, take a hand in the shaping of our lives. This lends a serious undertone to the tale even though it is lightly told. Kate Chopin neither ridicules nor condemns Alcée and his two women. She is a detached observer who nowhere raises a moral finger, not even where Alcée tries to make his wife stay away so that the affair he seems to plan can have free play. We might even say that the author suggests that the effects of his visit are beneficial to all: Bobinôt and Bibi gain as Calixta becomes more amiable; Clarisse feels a greater sense of freedom, and the two lovers are for the first time fully sexually awakened. But the conclusion that "every one was happy" is of course ambiguous. Mrs. Chopin may refuse to sit in judgment on morals, but she covers only one day and one storm and does not exclude the possibility of later misery. The emphasis is on the momentary joy of the amoral cosmic force, but the story's all-pervasive use of primordial symbolism strengthens the undertone of the serious, timeless aspect of Eros.

"The Storm" is about the tension between the male and the female, the assertive and the receptive principles. The immobile land is threatened by

From *Kate Chopin: A Critical Biography.* © 1969 by Per Seyersted.

the active river; the fields are exposed to rain and wind, as they are to the lightning which strikes through the intermediary of the tall trees. There is a constant play on the actions of opening or closing: Calixta unfastens "her white sacque at the throat" as she begins to shut the house; after riding in at the gate, Alcée tries to stay outside on the gallery, but is forced in by the storm; the rain threatens "to break an entrance and deluge them"; the heroine tries to keep the water out, and she is also afraid that the levee will give way. When we first see her, she is sewing—a popular metaphor of sexual intercourse. In connection with Alcée we are presented with such male symbols as the horse and the plow; another perfectly natural, yet very suggestive detail is the fact that the one piece of garment which he helps save from the rain is the trousers of the man whose privileges he shortly usurps. As for Calixta, her mouth is "a fountain of delight" and her flesh "a creamy lily" that is influenced by the sun.[2]

The story's diction is mostly fresh and honest; for example, Calixta is allowed to show "sensuous desire." But occasionally we find an excessive, old-fashioned, or stale phrase, such as "creamy lily," "well nigh," or "lips . . . to be tasted." Alcée's rather formal remark: "Let us hope, Calixta, that Bobinôt's got sense enough to come in out of a cyclone," may be functional, however, as an expression of how he tries to contain himself; and if we find a romantic ring in "swoon," we must add that D. H. Lawrence used the term, too, in connection with the same fundamental drives which, as Mrs. Chopin expresses it here, "contribute . . . to the undying life of the world."[3]

Though the story in one sense is Calixta's (she is nearly all the time in the foreground), it seems, with its Whitmanesque pervasive erotic atmosphere, dedicated to nature's undying urge rather than to any person. All details are suggestive of this central impulse. There is complete correspondence between theme, on the one hand, and setting, plot, and character, on the other. The elements of this piece are inextricably fused as the tale moves relentlessly forward, in one sustained, effortless sweep, toward the inescapable outcome of the cyclone. With a minimum of characterization this highly effective story gives a convincing picture of the figures—at once representative and individual—who are influenced by the storm. The tone greatly contributes to the artistic impact: detached and unsentimental, yet warm, and serenely free.

Artistically, "The Storm" is a first-rate story. It is important also for its daring. The frankness about sex of such books as *Madame Bovary* and *Nana* was of course slowly having an impact even on American fiction.

But with this tale, Kate Chopin not only outdistanced her compatriots, but also went a step beyond the Frenchmen. That her description of physical union is more open than theirs is a relatively minor point in this connection; what is important is its "happy," "healthy" quality.

Flaubert, who once owned that he had been obsessed by the word "adultery," makes Emma Bovary's amatory exploits into a frantic flight from dreariness; Zola sees those of Nana as the vile expressions of a degenerating heroine. Kate Chopin was not interested in the immoral in itself, but in life as it comes, in what she saw as natural—or certainly inevitable—expressions of universal Eros, inside or outside of marriage. She focuses here on sexuality as such, and to her, it is neither frantic nor base, but as "healthy" and beautiful as life itself. That "happy sex" should somehow be "indecent"—the answer Mary McCarthy gave when asked why she had described sex as "unhappy" in *The Group*—would be a completely foreign idea to the author of this story.[4] In "The Storm," there is exuberance and a cosmic joy and mystery as Alcée and Calixta become one with another and with elemental nature. With its organic quality, its erotic elation, and its frankness, the story almost makes its author an early D. H. Lawrence.

André Malraux has observed of Lawrence that he thought it more important to be a man than to be an individual. For Kate Chopin, the individuality of her heroines was more important than their femaleness. But to be a woman writer in her time meant almost the same as Virginia Woolf has said it did for Charlotte Brontë, that is, to be unable to avoid the "jerks" of a female "at war with her lot." When the author of *Jane Eyre* complains that "women . . . suffer from too rigid a restraint," it represents an indignation which prevents her from getting "her genius expressed whole and entire," Mrs. Woolf goes on. "It is fatal for any one who writes to think of their sex. . . . One must be woman-manly or man-womanly." It is particularly fatal for a female "in any way to speak consciously as a woman. . . . Anything written with that conscious bias is doomed to death. . . . There must be freedom and there must be peace."[5]

There is of course a fundamental female protest in *The Awakening*. But though what could be called her feminist stories are so greatly important in Kate Chopin's *œuvre*, they are rather few in number, and the rest of her writings show a detachment on the relationship between the sexes. The man-woman relationship of "The Storm"—the most intimate possible—is a crucial touchstone for objectivity, and Kate Chopin, who now had, on the one hand, the protest of *The Awakening* off her mind, and, on the other, literary success within her reach, here gives the impression of having achieved true freedom and real peace.

She is not consciously speaking as a woman, but as an individual. Even her previous writings had been free from misandry and from suggestions of either sex being superior to the other. In the present story, there is no trace of the covert bitterness of "Athénaïse," nor any complaint like Edna's that women learn so little of life. There is no antagonism or competition between Alcée and Calixta, no wilful domination in his manner or subservience in hers, even though he is higher up in society than she. In short, Mrs. Chopin appears to have achieved that thing—comparatively rare even today: to become a woman author who could write on the two sexes with a large degree of detachment and objectivity.

Notes to Part 3

1. *Song*, 4.3, and 4.5; CW, p. 595; Henry James, *Partial Portraits* (London, 1888), p. 249.

2. CW, pp. 592, 593, 595. The author's use of shrimps may represent a conscious allusion to the potency often denoted by sea foods. Mariequita in *The Awakening* also carries a basket of shrimps, and in "Athénaïse," the heroine eats shrimps together with Gouvernail.

3. CW, pp. 594, 595; see, for example, D. H. Lawrence, *Women in Love* (Penguin, 1960), p. 197.

4. Flaubert, *Novembre*, in *Oeuvres Complètes*, I (Paris, 1964), p. 257. According to *L'Express*, 28 Oct.–3 Nov., 1968, p. 42, Zola once wrote: "Tout geste sexuel qui n'a pas pour but la procréation est une infamie." Mary McCarthy in a TV interview, New York, Sept. 7, 1964.

5. André Malraux, Preface to *L'Amant de Lady Chatterley* (Paris, 1932); Charlotte Brontë, *Jane Eyre*, Ch. XII; Virginia Woolf, *A Room of One's Own* (New York, 1929), pp. 120, 121, 181, 182.

Chronology

1850	Catherine (Kate) O'Flaherty born in St. Louis on February 8, the second child of Thomas O'Flaherty of County Galway, Ireland, and Eliza Faris of St. Louis.
1855–1868	Attends St. Louis Academy of the Sacred Heart, with one year at the Academy of the Visitation.
1855	Her father dies in a railroad accident.
1863	Her beloved French-speaking great-grandmother dies; her half brother is captured by Union forces during the Civil War and dies of typhoid fever.
1867–1870	Keeps a commonplace book of essays, poems, diary entries, and copied extracts.
1869	Writes "Emancipation. A Life Fable," her first story.
1870	Marries Oscar Chopin, of Natchitoches Parish, Louisiana, whose French father had taken the family to Europe during the Civil War. Visits Cincinnati, Philadelphia, and New York, and tours Germany, Switzerland, and France on her wedding trip. Moves to New Orleans, where Oscar establishes a business.
1871–1879	Gives birth to five sons and a daughter.
1879	Moves to Cloutierville, in Natchitoches Parish, Louisiana, after Oscar closes his business because of hard times and buys a general store in Cloutierville.
1882	Oscar dies of malaria.
1883–1884	Has a romance with a local planter.
1884	Moves with her family to St. Louis.
1885	Her mother dies. Dr. Frederick Kolbenheyer, her obstetrician and a family friend, encourages her to write.
1888	Reads Maupassant. Begins "A No-Account Creole."

1889   First published story, "A Point at Issue!" appears in St. Louis *Post Dispatch.*

1890   First novel, *At Fault*, published privately. Completes second novel, *Young Dr. Gosse and Théo*, but later destroys it.

1890   Becomes active in St. Louis literary and cultural circles.

1891   Finishes "A No-Account Creole." Writes "Beyond the Bayou" and "After the Winter." Five stories appear in regional and national magazines, including *Youth's Companion* and *Harper's Young People.*

1892   Writes "Ripe Figs," "Ma'ame Pélagie," and "Désirée's Baby." "At the 'Cadian Ball" appears in *Two Tales.* Eight other stories published.

1893   Writes "In and Out of Old Natchitoches," "Madame Célestin's Divorce," "A Matter of Prejudice," "La Belle Zoraïde," and "A Lady of Bayou St. John." "Désirée's Baby" appears in the first issue of *Vogue.* Twelve other stories published. Travels to New York and Boston to seek a publisher for a novel and an anthology of stories.

1894   Writes "Lilacs," "The Kiss," and "Her Letters." Begins a diary, "Impressions," which she continues for two years. "The Story of an Hour" and "A Respectable Woman" appear in *Vogue*, "Tante Cat'rinette" in *Atlantic Monthly*, and "A No-Account Creole" and two other stories in *Century.* Three other stories published. Houghton Mifflin publishes *Bayou Folk*, an anthology of stories. Travels to a conference of the Western Association of Writers in Indiana.

1895   Writes "Athénaïse" and "The Falling in Love of Fedora." Twelve stories published.

1896   Writes "A Night in Acadie," "A Pair of Silk Stockings," "Nég Créol," and "A Vocation and a Voice." "Athénaïse" published in *Atlantic Monthly.* Five other stories published.

1897   Writes "A Morning Walk." Nine stories published. Way and Williams (of Chicago) publishes *A Night in Acadie*, an anthology of stories. Her grandmother, Athénaïse Charleville Faris, dies.

1897–1898 Writes *The Awakening.*

1898 Writes "The Storm."

1899 Story published in *Saturday Evening Post.* "In the Confidence of a Story-Writer," an essay, published by *Atlantic Monthly.* Herbert S. Stone publishes *The Awakening.*

1900 Writes "Charlie." Two stories published in *Vogue.* Herbert S. Stone cancels contract for *A Vocation and a Voice,* an anthology of stories.

1902 "A Vocation and a Voice" published in St. Louis *Mirror.* Last published story appears in *Youth's Companion.*

1904 Dies of a brain hemorrhage on August 22.

Selected Bibliography

Primary Works

Collections of Short Stories

Seyersted, Per, ed. *The Complete Works of Kate Chopin.* 2 vols. Baton Rouge: Louisiana State University Press, 1969. Includes both of Chopin's novels, her essays, poetry, and all but four of her known short stories.

———, and Emily Toth, eds. *A Kate Chopin Miscellany.* Natchitoches, LA: Northwestern State University Press, 1979. Includes the remaining four stories, additional poems, Chopin's diaries, letters, and other writings. Emily Toth, Per Seyersted, and Marilyn Bonnell are preparing a publication with new Chopin material.

Currently Available Paperback Anthologies of Short Stories

For a listing of which short stories are included in each of the following volumes, see Bernard Koloski. "The Anthologized Chopin: Kate Chopin's Stories in Yesterday's and Today's Anthologies." *Louisiana Literature* 11 (1994): 18–30.

The Awakening and Selected Short Stories by Kate Chopin. New York: Bantam, 1981.

Baym, Nina, ed. *The Awakening and Selected Short Stories by Kate Chopin.* New York: Modern Library, 1981.

Gilbert, Sandra M., ed. *The Awakening and Selected Stories by Kate Chopin.* New York: Penguin, 1984.

Leary, Lewis, ed. *The Awakening and Other Stories by Kate Chopin.* New York: Holt, 1970.

Robinson, Roxana, ed. *A Matter of Prejudice and Other Stories by Kate Chopin.* New York: Bantam, 1992.

Solomon, Barbara H., ed. *The Awakening and Selected Stories by Kate Chopin.* New York: Signet, 1976.

Taylor, Helen, ed. *Kate Chopin Portraits.* London: Women's Press, 1982.

Toth, Emily, ed. *A Vocation and a Voice: Stories by Kate Chopin.* New York: Penguin, 1991.

Secondary Works

Biographies

Rankin, Daniel. *Kate Chopin and Her Creole Stories.* Philadelphia: University of Pennsylvania Press, 1932.

Seyersted, Per. *Kate Chopin: A Critical Biography.* Baton Rouge: Louisiana State University Press, 1969.

Toth, Emily. *Kate Chopin.* New York: William Morrow, 1990.

Critical Studies

Abel, Elizabeth, Marianne Hirsch, and Elizabeth Langland, eds. *The Voyage In: Fictions of Female Development.* Hanover, NH: University Press of New England, 1983.

Bardot, Jean. *L'Influence Française dans la Vie et L'Œuvre de Kate Chopin.* Thèse de Doctorat, Université de Paris-IV, 1985–86.

Berthoff, Warner. *The Ferment of Realism: American Literature, 1884–1919.* 1965. New York: Cambridge University Press, 1981.

Bloom, Harold, ed. *Kate Chopin.* New York: Chelsea, 1987.

Bonner, Thomas, Jr. *The Kate Chopin Companion.* New York: Greenwood, 1988.

Boren, Lynda S., and Sara deSaussure Davis, eds. *Kate Chopin Reconsidered: Beyond the Bayou.* Baton Rouge: Louisiana State University Press, 1992.

Brooks, Van Wyck. *The Confident Years: 1855–1915.* New York: Dutton, 1952.

Christ, Carol P. *Diving Deep and Surfacing: Women Writers on Spiritual Quest.* Boston: Beacon, 1980.

Culley, Margaret, ed. *The Awakening: An Authoritative Text, Biographical and Historical Contexts, Criticism.* 2d ed. New York: Norton, 1994.

Dyer, Joyce. *The Awakening: A Novel of Beginnings.* New York: Twayne, 1993.

Elfenbein, Anna Shannon. *Women on the Color Line: Evolving Stereotypes and the Writings of George Washington Cable, Grace King, and Kate Chopin.* Charlottesville: University Press of Virginia, 1989.

Ewell, Barbara C. *Kate Chopin.* New York: Ungar, 1986.

Fryer, Judith. *The Faces of Eve: Women in the Nineteenth Century American Novel.* New York: Oxford University Press, 1976.

Gilbert, Sandra M., and Susan Gubar. *The Madwoman in the Attic: The Woman Writer and the Nineteenth-Century Literary Imagination.* New Haven: Yale University Press, 1979.

Jones, Anne Goodwyn. *Tomorrow Is Another Day: The Woman Writer in the South, 1859–1936.* Baton Rouge: Louisiana State University Press, 1981.

Koloski, Bernard, ed. *Approaches to Teaching Chopin's The Awakening.* New York: Modern Language Association of America, 1988.

Koppelman, Susan, ed. *Two Friends and Other Nineteenth-Century Lesbian Stories by American Women Writers.* New York: Meridian, 1994.

Lohafer, Susan. *Coming to Terms with the Short Story.* Baton Rouge: Louisiana State University Press, 1983.

Martin, Wendy, ed. *New Essays on The Awakening.* New York: Cambridge University Press, 1988.

Papke, Mary E. *Verging on the Abyss: The Social Fiction of Kate Chopin and Edith Wharton.* Westport, CT: Greenwood, 1990.

Pattee, Fred Lewis. *The Development of the American Short Story: An Historical Survey.* New York: Harper, 1923.

――――. *A History of American Literature Since 1870.* New York: Century, 1922.

Quinn, Arthur Hobson. *American Fiction: An Historical and Critical Survey.* New York: Appleton-Century, 1936.

Reilly, Joseph. *Of Books and Men.* New York: Messner, 1942.

Scott, Anne Firor. *The Southern Lady: From Pedestal to Politics, 1830–1930.* Chicago: University of Chicago Press, 1970.

Skaggs, Peggy. *Kate Chopin.* Boston: Twayne, 1985.

Spacks, Patricia Meyer. *The Female Imagination.* New York: Knopf, 1975.

Stein, Allen F. *After the Vows Were Spoken: Marriage in American Literary Realism.* Columbus: Ohio State University Press, 1984.

Taylor, Helen. *Gender, Race, and Region in the Writings of Grace King, Ruth McEnery Stuart, and Kate Chopin.* Baton Rouge: Louisiana State University Press, 1989.

Welter, Barbara. *Dimity Convictions: The American Woman in the Nineteenth Century.* Athens: Ohio University Press, 1976.

Wilson, Edmund. *Patriotic Gore: Studies in the Literature of the American Civil War.* 1962. Boston: Northeastern University Press, 1984.

Ziff, Larzer. *The American 1890s: Life and Times of a Lost Generation.* New York: Viking, 1966.

Articles and Parts of Books

Aaron, Daniel. "Per Seyersted: *Kate Chopin. A Critical Biography.*" *Edda* 71 (1971): 341–49.

Arms, George. "Kate Chopin's *The Awakening* in the Perspective of her Literary Career." In *Essays on American Literature in Honor of Jay B. Hubbell,* edited by Clarence Gohdes, 215–28. Durham, NC: Duke University Press, 1967.

Arner, Robert D. "Pride and Prejudice: Kate Chopin's 'Désirée's Baby.' " *Mississippi Quarterly* 25 (1972): 131–40.

――――. "Kate Chopin." Special issue of *Louisiana Studies* 14 (1975): 11–139.

――――. "Kate Chopin's Realism: 'At the 'Cadian Ball' and 'The Storm.' " *Markham Review* 2 (1970): 1–4.

Bardot, Jean. "French Creole Portraits: The Chopin Family from Natchitoches Parish." In *Perspectives on Kate Chopin: Proceedings from the Kate Chopin International Conference, April 6, 7, 8, 1989,* 25–36. Natchitoches, LA: Northwestern State University Press, 1992.

Selected Bibliography

Bender, Bert. "Kate Chopin's Lyrical Short Stories." *Studies in Short Fiction* 11 (1974): 257–66.

Blythe, Anne M. "Kate Chopin's 'Charlie.' " In *Kate Chopin Reconsidered: Beyond the Bayou*, edited by Lynda S. Boren and Sara deSaussure Davis, 207–15. Baton Rouge: Louisiana State University Press, 1992.

Bonner, Thomas, Jr. "Christianity and Catholicism in the Fiction of Kate Chopin." *The Southern Quarterly: A Journal of the Arts in the South* 20 (1982): 118–25.

————. "Kate Chopin: Tradition and the Moment." In *Southern Literature in Transition: Heritage and Promise*, edited by Philip and William Osborne Castille, 141–49. Memphis: Memphis State University Press, 1983.

Brown, Pearl L. "Kate Chopin's Fiction: Order and Disorder in a Stratified Society." *University of Mississippi Studies in English* 9 (1991): 119–34.

Davis, Sara deSaussure. "Chopin's Movement Toward Universal Myth." In *Kate Chopin Reconsidered: Beyond the Bayou*, edited by Lynda S. Boren and Sara deSaussure Davis, 199–206. Baton Rouge: Louisiana State University Press, 1992.

Dyer, Joyce. "Epiphanies through Nature in the Stories of Kate Chopin." *University of Dayton Review* 16 (1983): 75–81.

————. "Gouvernail, Kate Chopin's Sensitive Bachelor." *Southern Literary Journal* 14 (1981): 46–55.

————. "Kate Chopin's Sleeping Bruties." *Markham Review* 10 (1980): 10–15.

————. "The Restive Brute: The Symbolic Presentation of Repression and Sublimation in Kate Chopin's 'Fedora.' " *Studies in Short Fiction* 18 (1981): 261–65.

————. "Techniques of Distancing in the Fiction of Kate Chopin." *Southern Studies: An Interdisciplinary Journal of the South* 24 (1985): 69–81.

————, and Robert Emmett Monroe. "Texas and Texans in the Fiction of Kate Chopin." *Western American Literature* 20 (1985): 3–15.

Eble, Kenneth. "A Forgotten Novel: Kate Chopin's *The Awakening*." *Western Humanities Review* 10 (1956): 261–69. Rpt. in Culley, 188–93.

————. "Review of Per Seyersted, *Kate Chopin: A Critical Biography* and *The Complete Works of Kate Chopin*." *American Literary Realism* 4 (1971): 81–85.

Ellis, Nancy S. "Insistent Refrains and Self-Discovery: Accompanied Awakenings in Three Stories by Kate Chopin." In *Kate Chopin Reconsidered: Beyond the Bayou*, edited by Lynda S. Boren and Sara deSaussure Davis, 216–29. Baton Rouge: Louisiana State University Press, 1992.

Fluck, Winfried. "Tentative Transgressions: Kate Chopin's Fiction as a Mode of Symbolic Action." *Studies in American Fiction* 10 (1982): 151–71.

Gardiner, Elaine. " 'Ripe Figs': Kate Chopin in Miniature." *Modern Fiction Studies* 28 (1982): 379–82.

Gaudet, Marcia. "Kate Chopin and the Lore of Cane River's Creoles of Color." *Xavier Review* 6 (1986): 45–52.

Gilbert, Sandra M. "The Second Coming of Aphrodite: Kate Chopin's Fantasy of Desire." *The Kenyon Review* 5 (1983): 42–66.

Goldman, Arnold. "Life and Death in New Orleans." In *The American City: Literary and Cultural Perspectives,* edited by Graham Clarke. New York: St. Martin's, 1988.

Howell, Elmo. "Kate Chopin and the Creole Country." *Louisiana History* 20 (1979): 209–19.

———. "Kate Chopin and the Pull of Faith: A Note on 'Lilacs.' " *Southern Studies* 18 (1979): 103–9.

Kauffmann, Stanley. "The Really Lost Generation." *The New Republic,* 3 December 1966, 22, 37, 38.

Koloski, Bernard. "The Anthologized Chopin: Kate Chopin's Short Stories in Yesterday's and Today's Anthologies." *Louisiana Literature* 11 (1994): 18–30.

———. "The Swinburne Lines in *The Awakening.*" *American Literature* 45 (1974): 608–10.

Lattin, Patricia Hopkins. "Childbirth and Motherhood in *The Awakening* and in 'Athénaïse.' " In *Approaches to Teaching Chopin's The Awakening,* edited by Bernard Koloski, 40–46. New York: Modern Language Association of America, 1988.

———. "Kate Chopin's Repeating Characters." *Mississippi Quarterly* 33 (1980): 19–37.

———. "The Search for Self in Kate Chopin's Fiction: Simple Versus Complex Vision." *Southern Studies* 21 (1982): 222–35.

Leary, Lewis. "Kate Chopin, Liberationist?" *Southern Literary Journal* 3 (1970): 138–44.

McMahan, Elizabeth. " 'Nature's Decoy': Kate Chopin's Presentation of Women and Marriage in Her Short Fiction." *Turn-of-the-Century Women* 2 (1985): 32–35.

Miner, Madonne M. "Veiled Hints: An Affective Stylist's Reading of Kate Chopin's 'Story of an Hour.' " *Markham Review* 11 (1982): 29–32.

Mitchell, Angelyn. "Feminine Double Consciousness in Kate Chopin's 'The Story of an Hour.' " *CEAMagazine: A Journal of the College English Association, Middle Atlantic Group* 5 (1992): 59–64.

Moseley, Merritt. "Chopin and Mysticism." *Southern Studies: An Interdisciplinary Journal of the South* 25 (1986): 367–74.

Newman, Judie. "Kate Chopin: Short Fiction and the Art of Subversion." In *The Nineteenth-Century American Short Story,* edited by A. Robert Lee, 150–63. New York: Vision, 1985.

Papke, Mary E. "Chopin's Stories of Awakening." In *Approaches to Teaching Chopin's The Awakening,* edited by Bernard Koloski, 73–79. New York: Modern Language Association of America, 1988.

Selected Bibliography

Peel, Ellen. "Semiotic Subversion in 'Desiree's Baby.'" *American Literature* 62 (1990): 223–37.

Pope, Deborah. "Recent Developments in Kate Chopin Studies." *University of Mississippi Studies in English* 8 (1990): 254–58.

Potter, Richard H. "Negroes in the Fiction of Kate Chopin." *Louisiana History* 12 (1971): 41–58.

Ringe, Donald A. "Cane River World: Kate Chopin's *At Fault* and Related Stories." *Studies in American Fiction* 3 (1975): 157–66.

Rogers, Nancy E. "Echoes of George Sand in Kate Chopin." *Revue de Littérature Comparée* 1 (1983): 25–42.

Showalter, Elaine. "Chopin and American Women Writers." *Kate Chopin, The Awakening*, edited by Margo Culley, 2d ed., 311–20. New York: Norton, 1994.

Skaggs, Peggy. " 'The Man-Instinct of Possession': A Persistent Theme in Kate Chopin's Stories." *Louisiana Studies* 14 (1975): 177–85.

Toth, Emily. "Kate Chopin and Literary Convention: 'Desiree's Baby.'" *Southern Studies: An Interdisciplinary Journal of the South* 20 (1981): 201–8.

Valentine, Kristin B., and Janet Larsen Palmer. "The Rhetoric of Nineteenth-Century Feminism in Kate Chopin's 'A Pair of Silk Stockings.'" *Weber Studies: An Interdisciplinary Humanities Journal* 4 (1987): 59–67.

Wagner Martin, Linda. "Recent Books on Kate Chopin." *Mississippi Quarterly* 42 (1989): 193–96.

Wilson, Edmund. Foreword to *The Complete Works of Kate Chopin*, edited by Per Seyersted, 13–15, Vol. 1. 2 vols. Baton Rouge: Louisiana State University Press, 1969.

Wood, Ann Douglas. "The Literature of Impoverishment: the Woman Local Colorists in America 1865–1914." *Women's Studies* 1 (1972): 3–45.

Wymard, Eleanor B. "Kate Chopin: Her Existential Imagination." *Southern Studies: An Interdisciplinary Journal of the South* 19 (1980): 373–84.

Bibliographies

Bonner, Thomas, Jr. "Kate Chopin: An Annotated Bibliography." *Bulletin of Bibliography* 32 (1975): 101–5.

Gannon, Barbara C. "Kate Chopin: A Secondary Bibliography." *American Literary Realism, 1870–1910* 17 (1984): 124–29.

Inge, Tonette Bond. "Kate Chopin." In *American Women Writers: Bibliographical Essays*, edited by Maurice Duke et al., 47–69. Westport, CT: Greenwood, 1983.

Potter, Richard H. "Kate Chopin and Her Critics: An Annotated Checklist." *Missouri Historical Society Bulletin* 26 (1970): 306–17.

Seyersted, Per, and Emily Toth, eds. *A Kate Chopin Miscellany.* Natchitoches, LA: Northwestern State University Press, 1979.

Springer, Marlene, ed. *Edith Wharton and Kate Chopin: A Reference Guide.* Boston: G. K. Hall, 1976.

———. "Kate Chopin: A Reference Guide Updated." *Resources for American Literary Study* 11 (1981): 280–303.

Index

The Author

Bernard Koloski is professor of English at Mansfield University of Pennsylvania and has taught on the Fulbright program at Warsaw University and the Silesian University in Poland. He has published articles on Kate Chopin in *American Literature, Studies in American Fiction,* and *Louisiana Literature* and has edited *Approaches to Teaching Chopin's The Awakening,* published by the Modern Language Association of America. He has written also about Polish-American women writers.